UBU REPERTORY THEATER PUBLICATIONS

Individual plays:

Swimming Pools at War by Yves Navarre, 1982.

Night Just Before the Forest and *Struggle of the Dogs and the Black*, by Bernard–Marie Koltès, 1982.

The Fetishist by Michel Tournier, 1983.

The Office by Jean–Paul Aron, 1983.

Far From Hagondange and *Vater Land, the Country of our Fathers* by Jean–Paul Wenzel, 1984.

Deck Chairs by Madeleine Laik, 1984.

The Passport and *The Door* by Pierre Bourgeade, 1984.

The Showman by Andrée Chedid, 1984.

Madame Knipper's Journey to Eastern Prussia by Jean–Luc Lagarce, 1984.

Family Portrait by Denise Bonal, 1985; new edition, 1992.

Passengers by Daniel Besnehard, 1985.

Cabale by Enzo Cormann, 1985.

Enough is Enough by Protais Asseng, 1986.

Monsieur Thôgô–gnigni by Bernard Dadié, 1985.

The Glorious Destiny of Marshal Nnikon Nniku by Tchicaya U Tam'si, 1986.

Parentheses of Blood by Sony Labou Tansi, 1986.

Intelligence Powder by Kateb Yacine, 1986.

The Sea Between Us by Denise Chalem, 1986.

Country Landscapes by Jacques–Pierre Amette, 1986.

Nowhere and *A Man with Women* by Reine Bartève, 1987.

The White Bear by Daniel Besnehard, 1992.

The Best of Schools by Jean–Marie Besset, 1992.

Jock by Jean–Louis Bourdon, 1992.

A Tempest by Aimé Césaire, 1993 (new edition).

The Free Zone and *The Workroom* by Jean–Claude Grumberg, preface by Michael R. Marrus, 1993.

A Modest Proposal by Tilly, preface by Tom Bishop, 1994.

Ubu Repertory Theater:1982–1992, A bilingual illustrated history with personal statements by various playwrights and theater personalities, 1992.

*Distributed by Ubu Repertory Theater, 15 West 28th Street, New York, NY 10001. All other titles distributed by Theatre Communications Group, 355 Lexington Avenue, New York, NY 10017.

Anthologies:

Afrique I: New plays from the Congo, Ivory Coast, Senegal and Zaire, including *The Daughter of the Gods* by Abdou Anta Kâ, *Equatorium* by Maxime N'Debeka, *Lost Voices* by Diur N'Tumb, *The Second Ark* by Sony Labou Tansi, and *The Eye* by Bernard Zadi Zaourou. Preface by George C. Wolfe. 1987. (Out of print).

The Paris Stage: Recent Plays: *A Birthday Present for Stalin* by Jean Bouchaud, *The Rest Have Got It Wrong* by Jean–Michel Ribes, *The Sleepless City* by Jean Tardieu, *Trumpets of Death* by Tilly, and *The Neighbors* by Michel Vinaver. Preface by Catherine Temerson and Françoise Kourilsky. 1988.

Plays by Women: An International Anthology: *A Picture Perfect Sky* by Denise Bonal, *Jocasta* by Michèle Fabien, *The Girls from the Five and Ten* by Abla Farhoud, *You Have Come Back* by Fatima Gallaire–Bourega, and *Your Handsome Captain* by Simone Schwarz–Bart. Preface by Catherine Temerson and Françoise Kourilsky. 1988, 1991. (Out of print).

Gay Plays: An International Anthology: *The Function* by Jean–Marie Besset, *A Tower Near Paris* and *Grand Finale* by Copi, *Return of the Young Hippolytus* by Hervé Dupuis, *Ancient Boys* by Jean–Claude van Itallie, and *The Lives and Deaths of Miss Shakespeare* by Liliane Wouters. Preface by Catherine Temerson and Françoise Kourilsky. 1989, 1991.

Theater and Politics: An International Anthology: *Black Wedding Candles for Blessed Antigone* by Sylvain Bemba, *A Season in the Congo* by Aimé Césaire, *Burn River Burn* by Jean–Pol Fargeau, *Olympe and the Executioner* by Wendy Kesselman and *Mephisto,* adapted from Klaus Mann by Ariane Mnouchkine. Preface by Erika Munk. 1990.

Afrique II: New Plays from Madagascar, Mauritania and Togo including *The Legend of Wagadu as Seen by Sia Yatabere* by Moussa Diagana, *The Crossroads* by Josué Kossi Efoui, *The Herd* by Charlotte–Arrisoa Rafenomanjato, *The Prophet and the President* by Jean–Luc Raharimanana and *The Singing Tortoise* and *Yevi's Adventures in Monsterland* by Sénouvo Agbota Zinsou. Preface by Henry Louis Gates, Jr. 1991.

New French–Language Plays: *The Orphan Muses* by Michel Marc Bouchard (Quebec), *Fire's Daughters* by Ina Césaire (Martinique), *The Ship* by Michèle Césaire (Martinique), *Talk About Love!* by Paul Emond (Belgium), *That Old Black Magic* by Koffi Kwahulé (Ivory Coast). Preface by Rosette C. Lamont. 1993.

Plays by Women: An International Anthology. Book 2: *The Orphanage* by Reine Bartève (France), *Game of Patience* by Abla Farhoud (Quebec/Liban), *The Widow Dylemma* by Werewere Liking (Cameroon), *The Tropical Breeze Hotel* by Maryse Condé (Guadeloupe), *Beware the Heart* by Denise Bonal (France). Preface by Ntozake Shange. 1994.

Monologues: Plays from Martinique, France, Algeria, Quebec: *Another Story* by Julius Amédée Laou (Martinique), *Night Just Before The Forest* by Bernard-Marie Koltès (France), *The Sifter* by Michel Azama (France), *All It Takes Is Something Small* by Martine Drai (France), *Madame Bertin's Testimony* by Fatima Gallaire (Algeria), *Anatomy Lesson* by Larry Tremblay (Quebec). 1995.

Plays from Martinique,
France, Algeria, Quebec

monologues

UBU REPERTORY THEATER PUBLICATIONS
NEW YORK

CAUTION

Ubu Repertory Theater Publications
General Editors: Françoise Kourilsky, Cristina Strempel, Catherine Temerson
Distributed by Theatre Communications Group, 355 Lexington Avenue, New York, NY 10017

Price: $15.95
Printed in the United States of America 1995
Library of Congress Catalog Card Number: 94-62160
ISBN 0-913745-44-8

The publication of this book was made possible, in part, by grants from the Cultural Services of the French Embassy, New York, the Quebec Government House, New York, and the Martinique Promotion Bureau.

CONTENTS

Julius Amédée Laou

Another Story

Translated from the French by
Richard Miller

UBU REPERTORY THEATER PUBLICATIONS
NEW YORK

Julius Amédée Laou was born in Paris in 1950. His family is from Martinique. After studying architecture at the Ecole des Beaux-Arts in Paris, he started writing and directing for the stage and screen. He has written and directed three films: *Solitaire à micro ouvert,* the prize-winning short at the 1984 Venice Film Festival, was shown twice on French television as was his second short, *Mélodie de brumes à Paris* (1985). His feature film, *La vieille quimboiseuse et le majordome,* was awarded prizes at the 1987 Festival de la Francophonie; it was shown commercially in Paris for several months and on Channel Four, in England, in 1988 and 1990. In 1982, Laou co-founded and directed a Paris theater company made up of African and Caribbean actors, La Compagnie des Griots d'Aujourd'hui; the group premiered his first play the same year, *Ne m'appelez jamais nègre.* His second play, *Folie ordinaire d'une fille de Cham* was premiered at the Théâtre de la Bastille in 1984; it later toured Europe, was performed in translation in Germany and Sweden, and was filmed by Jean Rouch. *Sonate en Solitude Majeure* was premiered by Laou's theater group in 1986 and later toured France. His two subsequent plays, *La fin du rêve du roi Narmer* and *Les Trompettes de la renommée,* were published by Editions des Quatre-Vents in 1992. *Another Story* was commissioned and produced by the 1992 "Arts au Soleil" Festival in Boulogne; it has since been performed by several theater groups in a number of French cities. Julius Amédée Laou presently lives in Martinique.

Richard Miller has translated many works of fiction and non-fiction, from Balzac to Barthes, as well as a number of plays for Ubu Repertory Theater. His translations of Aimé Césaire's *A Tempest,* Paul Emond's *Talk About Love!* and Tilly's *A Modest Proposal,* were staged at Ubu in 1991, 1993 and 1994 respectively. He has recently translated *Women and Men* by Bernard-Henri Lévy and Françoise Giroud, and is currently translating a biography of Yves Saint Laurent. He presently lives in Paris.

Another Story, in Richard Miller's translation, had its American premiere at Ubu Repertory Theater, 15 West 28th Street, New York, NY 10001, on March 14, 1995.

Director...**Françoise Kourilsky**
Set Designer...**Watoku Ueno**
Lighting Designer...**Greg MacPherson**
Costume Designer...**Carol Ann Pelletier**
Music composed and performed by..........................**Genji Ito**

CAST, IN ORDER OF APPEARANCE

Sawa...**Erika L. Heard**
Abraham Ben Israel....**Robert Morgan**
Adelaide Beaulieu...**La Tonya Borsay**
Mory Haidara....**Andréa Smith**

Special appearance by **Duane McLaughlin** as *Pangale Keita*

Produced by **Ubu Repertory Theater**
Françoise Kourilksy, *Artistic Director*

AUTHOR'S NOTE

Transitory world...world of transition...amnesias, memories shift from death to life...world of vibrant life—yes, vibrant, living world! Our mortal world...this passing world is ours, it bears the marks, the memory, the traces of sufferings, the lessons of life, the recurring pain, again and again, turning and returning.

World of overt and hidden horrors, world of small, passing pleasures that become a part of us... World in which Histories, Civilizations, have been created, shot through with all the madness of blood, of the perverse lies of men who have blithely traded their visions of love for the mocking toys of death, for puny power and privilege; intrigues...sacrifices to hatred.

They flee in terror from the sight of truth... Sometimes, for fleeting and fragile moments, they venture upon tenuous, inner paths in the more powerful silence that calls out to them, endlessly...but they do not want to hear.

And a few short hours and death calls them and they heed... Their vanities, their contemptible deeds, their cowardice, their ambitions, all those weaknesses, the weight of their lives, sucks them down into the depths... And just before death they grow deaf unto tears...justifying their acts as erroneous reasons of state, their wicked yearnings! ...true reasons to hate! ... to hate themselves!

Far far from this life that turns and turns, that turns in this endless death seeking forever its brightest, fairest light...

JULIUS AMEDEE LAOU

CHARACTERS

SAWA, *A young West-Indian girl witnessing the arrival of Columbus's three caravels and, along with the other inhabitants of her village, preparing to greet the new arrivals.*

ABRAHAM BEN ISRAEL, *A young Marrano, a Spanish Jew, raised by the monks following his family's massacre by the Inquisition. The soldiers who had murdered them left him at a monastery when he was five years old. At nineteen Abraham Ben Israel, whose name had been changed to Juan Jose Martinez, was kidnapped by strangers sent by the King and an admiral named Columbus; the men were in a hurry and filled with anxiety. They took him to a boat where he was to be a passenger on a long trip.*

ADELAIDE BEAULIEU, *A young black house slave at a mansion in Martinique, she tends the baby Charles, the son of Master Bartholomew Bassanville and his wife, Mathilde, her owners.*

MORY HAIDARA, *A nobleman of the Mali Empire, a member of the Council of Wise Men, an Initiate, a Master Blacksmith, a Keeper of Secrets and Knowledge, he is a cultivated, intelligent, powerful man. With his fellows on the Council, he had deposed the ruler, the wicked Sangare, and the expected reprisals had been carried out. Captured by his enemy, he is sold to the white slavers who prey along the coast.*

All of the characters who speak to us are dead. They have returned to visit us...to give an account... They speak from beyond their deaths, from a time before or after their lives, after their parts have been played, after the curtain has fallen.

They are brought together to speak openly, to commune with us.

I.

*Sawa, a young Taino Indian, appears; she tells of a day
when she and her companions first caught sight of the giant
boats in the distance.*

SAWA: I was playing in the water with Ksaimo, who was catching fish for supper between kissing me, many kisses for Sawa,
I was playing at his side, happy just to come up against his
skin, to touch him, there were already three huge crabs on
the beach, the ones everybody likes.

I'm Sawa. The water was soft and gentle against our skin. I
was playing in the water with Ksaimo, handsome Ksaimo, and
the children were playing too, watching us together, laughing, happy, and the women were singing as they gathered
mangoes, bread-fruit, papayas, plucking their parrots. Ksaimo
is the lover I like best, my favorite, the one who makes me cry
out the loudest, all the children like him too, almost as much
as the women do, that's what they all call him: "Ksaimo-who-
makes-the-women-cry-out-loud," and I'm happy with him.

We were playing in the water, I was shouting myself, the happy
children were splashing and swimming and washing themselves—when a cry like I'd never heard before from a woman's
throat seemed to tear the air apart, a cry that rang in our
heads, the sound of it pulled me down to earth and I looked
back at them standing there, they were all standing there on
the beach, frozen, terrified, and for a moment I didn't understand, I thought maybe the Caniyas were attacking, everyone
I knew was just standing there motionless, terrified of what
they were seeing somewhere in the distance, something that
made them all stare.

Even Payo had fallen silent, just staring out to sea, a look of horror on her face, and I didn't dare turn to look too. Ksaimo rose up in the water, it had grown cold, and he stared out at the monster on the horizon, so calmly, and then he began to smile, he was the only one who looked at the monster without flinching, looking at it straight on, calmly, but then, Ksaimo is always calm after he's been playing with a woman, I could feel his calm like courage in my hands, I could feel it through my body.

In Ksaimo's arms nothing frightened me, the sight the others were seeing had no power to frighten me, and I slowly turned toward that impossible supernatural thing, that image from the underworld, risen out of some nightmare long forgotten, those three giant dugouts, immense canoes with great sails painted and striped, spread out like a threat on the horizon, the canoes of giants who had journeyed from their world to ours for some strange, unknown, disturbing reason, had they come to hunt us, to slaughter us—had they run out of meat?

I was calm, like Ksaimo, but all the same I pressed up closer to him. Old Maayati had ordered the shell horns to be blown, the drums to beat, he had called for all to assemble in the sacred circle. And soon all the adults were there and all the children were trembling in the huts, and then Old Maayati spoke to us, saying: "Three giant canoes with sails have come from the nether world of the demons and their crews will soon come ashore and fall upon us, as did the Agailaitwi, those flying devils with their murderous fire. These creatures have come for tribute, they seek offerings and fresh meat, women and precious stones, our fine fresh vegetables and our fruits, and before the moon sets another time they will scratch with their claws into our warm sands, they will leave their bloody marks behind them, their violence, for it is written in the winds. If we are to remain alive we must use all our craft! These monsters, who have left their own world for our offerings—and hear this, for it is the truth I speak!—will always want more, they will always want greater and further sacrifices, they will call for more offerings, and if our people are to live on we must yield to them, if our children are to grow to know life! Our most beautiful women will be offered to the devils, some of the strongest and handsomest of our men will be given them for their games, but we cannot fall back, we must not appear to be too crafty, for the devils know. So we must sacrifice, we must sacrifice that we may live, we must sacrifice and await their death and protect ourselves, we must sacrifice to them and cover the beach with gifts of welcome, we must coax them to assuage their boundless, destructive, murderous appetites."

And Old Maayati spoke on: "And these giants from far away, from far below, these monsters who seek blood and women, who want for themselves all things that are man's—they crave such things only to destroy them, to devour them, to glut themselves with them! No, no, never! Still we must pile the beach high with offerings. You, who are to be the sacrifice, you Chosen Ones who will live henceforth eternal with the Gods and with the Quick, go now and prepare yourselves! Yes, for you, the Quick, I have chosen Taqxiana as the next chief for his wisdom and his strength, for he is young and he will replace me, and he is brave and will be for you what I have been! Go then and hide yourselves in the forest, preserve our clan, preserve our village and our Gods!"

Thus spoke Maayati, and he chose the children and the women and the men for Sacrifice to save our clan, the children to be given as meat to feed the famished giants who will roast them first, they were there, silent, not laughing; the women handed over for their pleasure, as toys; the men to be game for the killing, for their devil games, to fight together for their amusement; death and laughter, the stakes in the mortal games these devils prize so highly.

And they were to be given jewels, stones, goods for their vanity and comfort, and the fruits and vegetables to eat until they are able to eat no more, until they groan and vomit from eating. The devils love a feast, they smack their lips and growl as they feed, we know, until finally, perhaps, they collapse, and then we will slay them!

You who go to take refuge in the forest, you the Quick, you will keep watch on them until they succumb to sleep, their last sleep! You will kill them when the time is ripe, you will lie in wait.

Each had his place then, the Quick had fled and were already hidden deep among the trees. And the Chosen Ones had taken up their places—I, Sawa, was a Chosen One, the most beautiful to be chosen for the pleasure of the giants and I was ready, naked there on the beach for their pleasure, an eternal Sacrifice, and my thoughts were all of Ksaimo, who had gone into the forest to spy upon them, to wait there to kill them.

The Quick had gone—their world was now no longer mine, the women, men and children who had gone to hide themselves among the trees. Here on the shore, waiting here, prepared to meet the giants, we were the Chosen Ones, we were now blessed, we already walked on the true path that leads to the village of the Gods, and now we stood here on the flower-strewn beach surrounded with the best of our fruits, the best of our produce, with tender children fresh for the roasting, and we all waited, the men prepared to die for the devils' eyes, ready to enter the eternal village.

With Old Maayati's guidance we will perish under the teeth

of the giants. In the forest the new chief of the Quick, the strong Taqxiana, peers from his hiding place to watch the monsters' arrival, to see how they will act, and we women stand ready to play this wicked game, honored to be Chosen Ones, to be sacrificed because we are the most beautiful, we stand laughing, knowing that the end of the devils' games must be our death, laughing, glad that soon we will be with the Gods, eternal as they are.

Never again will Ksaimo hold me in his arms. All the most beautiful women chosen by the Gods are here to be sacrificed to uphold the Laws. And our names, our bodies, will become the stuff of legend, and the devils will fall down dead at the sight of our beauty, and we will live forever in beauty through-out all eternity, remembered by the Quick as the most beau-tiful, remembered as the Glorious Sacrifices, the Chosen Ones. We shall be beautiful as long as man remembers, as long as our people will remember, our happy people who will forever adore my body, who will adore me as a Goddess triumphant over evil spirits, over devils!

There they stand, the giant canoes, motionless, there we stand on the shore waiting for our death. Huge dugouts, filling the sky out there, hiding the sun, the canoes of monsters from the devil land, lying silent and becalmed, watching back at us, lifeless and cold. The fruits, the vegetables, the children, the women, Old Maayati our chief is an offering too, the men wait in fear and trembling, in horror, for the monsters seem to be asleep, there is death in our fear, there are horrors and terror and blood, and there is the joy of the Chosen Ones to be sacrificed for eternity.

And I a goddess frozen in my beauty in the memories of all who will live after me, touched by my gift of myself, to be praised to the end of time. And the spirits of the monsters stand ready too, waiting out there, their silent and motion-less canoes hang heavy on the horizon, the thunder does not speak, the Gods give no sign, there is only silence! Among us no one breathes, our eyes, our ears, our terror, time—everything is suspended, everything stands still, and then...

Like spiders in giant webs they climb down and down, the sails billow out and fall, like tiny dwarfs they come out all covered in strange raiment...so small...are the giants then waiting somewhere else, are they hiding from us?

The dwarfs scurry about, the giants' slaves who make the dugouts move, they crawl down into smaller canoes that have been lowered into the sea, now they're really coming, that much we know, to tell us of the giants, they will announce their awakening, they will tell us of our death, they will tell us their wishes and commands, they will select the Chosen Ones for the first games, the first feast.

Now they paddle toward us with determination, all so strangely pale, some of them are gray and green, some are swarthy red, some pale gray, the one in front has a face the color of the pus from putrid sores. And on the beach of the Chosen Ones a silence has fallen, all sound has been sucked up by the sight of the devils, soon with our Gods we will be coming to save the Quick, we will wait!

The evil dwarfs are drawing closer! They are coming closer...they are almost the same size, they are smaller than we Men... They come even closer, and now they leap from their canoes and come together in a bunch, they are clumsy and gross, as they move, and now the monsters stumble and wade toward us, they stumble as they advance toward us through the water, their leader ahead of them, they are covered with a strange and horrible skin that may be raiment but still strange, and their faces and what some of them use for hands, are bare and uncovered, and the rest of their bodies is covered with a kind of skin, this strange colored fabric.

And out there, surely, out there on the great hulks the giants must be hiding... But we are not afraid, we are waiting to enter the village of the Gods, and so they draw near in silence, and nearer... We are not afraid, we stand ready in silence for our deaths, watched over by the Quick, standing beautiful for them, for them to remember. There, behind us, there the Quick are watching, and the Gods are pleased.

The devils come toward us and we do not move, in our dream we watch them, in our nightmare... Now their chief sets foot on our shore, the things he has for hands stretch out to us. They are filthy, they stink, there is a horrid smell. And at the stench many of the Sacrificial Ones, with Old Maayati, seem to fall back, and recover, the women chosen to die as offerings to the Gods move forward, the children fall silent, the men await death. The Sacrificial Ones, even the vegetables and fruit, shrink and shrivel at the horrible smell of filth from the monsters. And behind us the Quick stand frozen, fascinated, staring beyond the circle of Gods to the shore of death, watching the Sacrificial Ones advance smiling toward the evil dwarfs, the servants of the sleeping giants, and the children cry at their filthy odor.

We are still comforted that they have not appeared, we are awaiting the teeth of death, and finally we too move forward, smiling, ready to Sacrifice for the Quick, and then death opens its arms to us, covered with those strange scales, and we go forward in joy, joyfully, we Sacrificial Chosen Ones, to sleep in the arms of the Gods through all eternity, and we fall into their arms as offerings, we await their evil spells, our death.

And the monsters have set foot on our land to devour it and

we move forward to them with smiles, our plans hidden from them, joyful, to captivate them. And they trample our sand, and what they use for hands stretch out to us to steal, to kill, to burn, to rape, to take us, and we have done our best to welcome them with our offerings and our smiles, so that they may spare our Gods and our Quick.

II

Abraham Ben Israel returns, he tells of the voyage bearing him toward an unknown land to the east of the Indies, to the virgin lands of the Great Khan, a passenger on the Admiral's flagship.

ABRAHAM BEN ISRAEL: I had been playing my flute, idly, lying on the foredeck of the Admiral's ship, I had been half asleep, dreaming on a moving ocean, and then I woke up, and from the dark secret depths of the damp hull I heard strange sounds, sounds that seemed to come from my parched childhood, the sound of lost songs, of words, of a language long buried and forgotten and now singing out with joy, the songs my father had sung, the songs my uncles had sung, the songs of all the grown-ups standing around me...

My name is Juan Jose Martinez, I was shut up in a monastery when I was five years old, after my parents' death, I am the only survivor... They all screamed, I can remember that, when they took them away, they all screamed, my mother threw herself on top of me to hide me, to protect me, she was desperate, screaming...and the soldiers ran her through...there I lay, underneath her, in her blood, I lay there until the soldiers pulled me up and handed me over to the monks, to the monastery where I grew up in the blood and the screams of my mother, and I didn't really learn... They said I was simple-minded, and I used to play all day in the courtyards, in the corridors, in the chapels and refectory, I used to hide in play, I would dance on the grass and roll about in the flower beds and the monks used to laugh, they were all very fond of me, from the Grand Abbot, Alfonso, down to the newly-arrived novices, they were all fond of me, and in my play, in my laughter, they could all hear my mother's screams and see her blood.

All the brothers were fond of me, until the day when the King's envoy, men from King Ferdinand the Catholic, came into the refectory to get me, Pinzon, the Admiral's right-hand man, was with them, and Don Abravanel the Jew, the Grand Treasurer of the Realm, and other men who had come from His Most Catholic Majesty King Ferdinand to take me away that 30th of July in the year of our disgrace 1492, in those dark days when all the Jews were being expelled from Spain.

They dressed me up to take me away, they no longer called me Juan Jose, these strangers, they called me Abraham, and as I rode along in their midst the name made me want to cry, it was as though my mother were speaking to me, as though I could hear my father calling to me in a dream, as though I could see them there among these men who had brought them and their voices back to me. And we travelled and travelled, and they spoke in another tongue, not like the Spanish that I knew, in a language that I seemed to hold in my heart, in the tongue of my dead parents, a strange tongue, and I remembered the tears and the laughter mingled with their whispered words and I could hear the sound of my father's name and the names of my uncles and the name of my mother, and they were talking about my ancestors and about the great men of my people, about the famous and the dead.

And again Don Abravanel, speaking softly, said my name, "Abraham Ben Israel," and he said "You are a Jew, Abraham Ben Israel, you are a Jew," and he repeated it to me again and again, in my ear, those words, the name my mother had called me... My mother! In my ear then they whispered to me of my uncles and of my father, of a plan, of the search for another land, of setting out for the Indies to find the ten lost tribes of Israel, to find our people there, in freedom, our people who might be searching for us too, far away there.

And the great ships stood at the quayside and I listened to the story of my family... And those men who had seen to it that memory, that speech, would live on, those men brought me there with their kind whispers as the soldiers before had carried me in haste, anxious and relieved. And now I was far from communions, far from the dark cloisters and the vespers, far from the penances and all the blood drowning the voice of the mother who was searching for me, calling to me... And they came down from the foredeck of the Admiral's ship to take me up, they bore me up into this large inner cabin, concealed, hidden away, secret, all painted, I can remember it now, like our house when I was a child, before.

The seven-branched candelabra, the menorah, stood there in the center, now it is mine, now I am a Jew, the same as the one the soldiers had smashed and thrown to the ground, swearing as they trampled it, my father trying to pick it up, their weapons striking down at him, cutting into his head, into his flesh, into his bones, everywhere, and my mother's screams, they had run her through with their spears, with their swords, through my mother's screams.

And I had slept beneath her, dead, she had spoken to me, my sisters had cried out as the men tore into them, and I lay sleeping in the whispers and the blood, in my mother's words...today I can hear them more clearly: Abraham, you are a Jew, never forget the words of your dead mother, Abraham Ben Israel, you are a Jew, my dead mother was saying that.

We left port soon after the fast of Tisha b'Av of the Psalms of King David. I came down into the hold where they were all praying and reading and they spoke to me of the great rabbi Haim Ben Israel, my father, and of Isaac Scholem and Elie Ben Israel, my grandfathers, and of him who had brought light into the darkness of his people, of him who was called

Jacob Ben Asher, my great-grandfather, the elder who had lit the darkness of my people with prayer, beloved in the secret silence of our hidden and buried nights, our concealed, insulted, burned and trampled faith.

I heard my mother, I heard her sobbing on my body, "You are a Jew, Abraham, you are Abraham Ben Israel, a Jew." And then I found the Book and the Scripture, the reason of my faith, and I read for them all, I read as I had never ceased to read...and, silently, they listened as I read the Psalms, the Texts, the words that spoke to me, that spoke to all us Jews, hidden in our cellars.

At midnight the anchor was raised at the end of the rite of the destruction of the Temples, I was swimming in the Word, rediscovered, read and spoken! The Word that has given me back unspoiled my father's tears, that had been clear as my living father's gaze. I came last to stand before the refound Wall, I returned to the Wall to weep, to hope at last, at last free to seek...my mother's eyes, her tears...

After the Word, they all introduced themselves, all of them, by their true names of our true faith: Jose Manuel Jimenez, the Map Maker, that good devout Christian on the bridge, was here our Rabbi, Moshe Ha-Cohen, and they all knew me, they all knew my story, all but me, and they gave it back to me, to my father and mother and children to come in the new free land.

We raised anchor on that day, that last day for the Spanish Jews, at the last minute before the land became a forbidden land. And we left, Jews, with a captain of our own faith, for the New Land, East of the Indies, for the virgin lands unknown to Christians and Western Jews, we went to meet the Great Khan, to negotiate with him in secret my people's peace, the peace of the future immigrants.

A New World...seeking the Tribes of Israel lost since the beginning of time, seeking them always elsewhere, and one day we will find them, in some other world... In the final minutes we left, filled with awe, feverish, close-pressed in the final hour of the Expulsion of the Spanish Jews, in those last minutes of that infamous edict of Their Most Catholic Majesties King Ferdinand and Queen Isabella of Spain, stained with treachery and hatred and unreason.

Eyes turned away, driven from us, conversos, marranos, believing Jews, setting forth on every road in the exodus of faith, for a pound of bread the Christians demanded an equal weight of gold! Our expulsion was to mean their misfortune... So great a kingdom, to pursue and despoil and murder its own children, its doctors, its teachers, its merchants, its philosophers, must surely bring down upon itself much long-suffering! Wherever there are Jews, there is a way of the cross!

In the last minutes of the Edict, at night, we left the harbor of the forbidden land to seek a new land, not a promised land but a land promising peace for that people, my people, endlessly wandering through the storms of hatred that have raged throughout all time to kill us, to fall upon us.

One of the greatest of men, the greatest of captains, leads us, he is of our faith, of our customs, of our heart, a Jew of an Old House, a secret house, concealed beneath a devout, most Christian man bold in the sun of the Most Catholic Kings and Queens of Spain, a Jew at heart, a Jew whose mother and father were Jews like me, Abraham Ben Israel, like my father and my mother... A Jew in faith beneath the moon, hidden like the rest in his demeanor, this Jewish captain Columbus, the inspired protector of our secrets and our fate. As a navigator he knows all the numbers that can lead us to where our people and all Mankind must journey in the eyes of God and of history. He knows the numbers and he leads us under their protection, the numbers handed down by the Wise Men, by the Masters of the Cabala, the mathematicians, the map-makers, the astronomers, they are bearing us to a new world, a free world, a world far from fear where we will in silence set up our Tables, the Menorah.

The Christians surround us and we commune with them, even outside Spanish waters we continue to fear them, the lowliest Christian ship's boy can put his captain, the most brilliant of men, to the stake, deliver men to death, to the Inquisition, for fear is all-powerful, all-powerful the crime of hatred, jealousy, of informing! We are Jews in their midst, Christians set forth to convert for gold, to enslave, to exploit, to confess for power, to sell indulgences! Entry to the Kingdom of God is to be bought with the sound of silver, growing ever richer on the credulity of their flock, evangelizing for gold, gold, always more gold!

Before descending from our barks and walking on the sands we required the promised sign from God, the portent, Jew, in the skies, and the hour and the day were ours! We had seen the eloquent sign, great for the glory of God, of our Faith! We Jews had come to this land on this very glorious day foretold and for centuries proclaimed, on Hoshanah Rabah, we had come minutes before Simhath Torah, on the seventh night of Sukkoth, on the holy night of forgiveness, at the end of Kippur, at the last chance, the very last, when the Shofar sounds at the reading of the Book of Psalms and the prayers, at this very shining moment God had put aside for the Jews' first setting foot upon the New Land.

Rodrigo de Triana, a Christian, was the first to shout it from the mast: "Land ho!", the first on that clear morning of the 20th of Tishri in the year 5253 of our era, the 11th of October 1492 for the Christians. The 21st of Tishri, and the next day we set foot on land, walking into a better tomorrow... And here our people will come into the strong and peaceful place set aside for them in the future of the New World! This fine great holy day coinciding with our arrival must mean great prosperity for my people in these new lands, as we await the arrival of the Great Khan!

Men, women and children stand on the shore, motionless, standing there before us covered with flowers, bearing food, silent, their eyes fixed upon us. Can they be the ten lost tribes of Israel who stand gazing upon us, who await us? Whoever they are, we move forward to these new men, our hands stretched out to give, to share, to rediscover justice and peace, that they may be at last given unto us all!

III

*Adelaide Beaulieu appears and tells us of the strange events
that occurred on the Bassanville plantation in Martinique.
Adelaide, a house slave, was nurse to the infant Charles.*

ADELAIDE BEAULIEU: I was with Charles, Master's little
boy, playing with the child, I had been nursing him, and then
Master Barthelemy came in, he just lifted me by the waist and
threw me down, down to the floor, and he...he took me there,
right in front of the child, he just stared at us, he was barely
three months old, he just watched his father there on top of
me, he didn't make a sound, and me, letting him, I didn't
make a sound either.

And then...Master let me go, and he went and bent down over
his child, staring down into his eyes, Master looked down at
Charles in such a strange way, and he just sat there, anxious,
and quiet, and I was afraid, and then, little by little, at first I
didn't understand, I could see the hatred, the anger, start to
burn in Master's eyes, and then, all of a sudden, just like an
animal, he picked up the child in one hand as if to kill him,
and he shook him, and the child cried out, and Master yelling
like a man possessed: "A mulatto, a mulatto! The boy's a
mulatto, he's not mine! He's worse than a devil's child, he's
a mulatto child, my wife's been with a negro, a mulatto, it's
not mine, it's a negro's!"

And I screamed out, for him to have pity, "Have pity on that
child," I screamed, "have pity on baby Charles, have pity, let
him have some air, have pity, Master, he's your son, you got
to believe that, don't blaspheme, Master."

But then he left, he went out with the wrath of the devil in
his heart looking for Mistress, looking for his wife Mathilde,
and the poor thing couldn't say a word, he came dragging

her by the hair, he dragged her, screaming, back to the child, with me still there on the floor all sweat and blood and him yelling like a crazy man.

And then all the slaves came running up from all over, terrified, I could see them outside in the yard, I could see them running around like the devil was after them, frightened at what was happening, and then running off again to hide somewhere, wherever they could find, hiding from our Master and his madness, Master Barthelemy, blind with his rage, dragging his wife behind him on the floor, and he cut into her, she was gushing blood, and he led her like a lamb to the slaughter, like a sacrifice, cutting into the body of his wife, her pale body, white as linen cloth...

And he grabbed the machete of Old Sideon, and he cut up her living body right there in front of the child, right in front of me, and all the slaves watching, their eyes shining with fear, all the field slaves running by the window on their way to hide and looking in without stopping, their eyes like flashes of lightning, and me dying of pain, screaming out, afraid for the child.

And he just cut her up right in front of me, so calm, so careful, in his wrath, his wife, whom he was supposed to love so much: "Who's the bastard's father, who is it? The negro! My pure race, my superior blood, it can't bring forth a devil's child, a son of Satan, thus saith our Lord!" And Master was still looking for the answer in the pieces of his wife's body he lifted up in his bloody hands, the wife he'd loved so well, the pieces of the dead Mistress, big lumps of bleeding flesh there in my poor crazy Master's hands, the beloved Master, his eyes all bloodshot and him raving like that all alone over the pieces of his wife, the wife he'd loved so well, her lying dead from Old Sideon's machete and by her husband's hand, a mute, consenting death, dead in silence, not ever understanding the reason, the secret, the misunderstanding that had killed her, dead for some dark reason, some dark law, some dark ceremony.

All covered in blood, Master fell down on the pieces of his wife's body strewn all around the floor... He just looked up at me then with his red crazy eyes, he didn't seem to understand, and then he took baby Charles up in his hands to cut him up too, like he had Miss Mathilde before with Old Sideon's sharp machete.

Suddenly Big Seraphin, the cane cutter, the slave, crazed, violent Seraphin, was standing there in the window, with Master's gun in his hands, and for a bit he just stood there and looked in at him, staring in at him, a long long moment, and him with his blood-red eyes, the machete raised up, staring back at Seraphin there in the window, ready to cut into baby Charles who was just lying there all quiet, like frozen, watching and lucid, and then the gun went off and our master—God save him!—he fell down dead, his chest was blown open like a duck that's been hit by a shotgun shell, he fell face down, and baby Charles beneath him in the bloody guts strewn over the floor, the poor baby gasping out for breath, struggling to stay alive, struggling under dead Master's body there with his chest all blown apart by Seraphin's gun.
And I grabbed up the child, he didn't cry, he was fighting strong to live, that child looked straight at me, he decided to stay alive to live his life, strong among his own, among all those dead! Under the bodies, in the blood, lying with the innards of his dead parents, still he didn't cry, his eyes seemed almost calm, and commanding, knowing, stubborn, strong. The child's eyes ordered me to take him outside, and Seraphin took him up and he went off with him in his arms, laughing, shouting out, dancing with joy, and I could hear them both laughing, it's true, it's true, I'm telling the truth, I saw them

all going off to the Land of Freed Slaves.

Oh Free Black World, a new Prince is come, and your history will never tell of him! Freed black Africans, free black Africans, a new Prince is coming! Far away from the burning planta-tions, far away from the raped women and the pillaged lands, in the Hill Kingdom where the Great Lords of Night live, Free Blacks of Martinique, Americas and Africa, our princes are alive, they run, they hide, powerful, clever and laughing, per-haps the saviors of some future century.

They wait on the outskirts of the white men's history, out-side their silent, false stories, made to kill us, far from the whips, the dogs, the sugar canes and the humiliation! They will bring life, make us see the beauty of our world, a power-ful and majestic vision.

So I went back to the house and I set fire to it, I shouted to them all as they stood by, trembling: "Tell everyone that the house caught fire by accident, killing our Master, Master Barthelemy whom we all loved, tell that it was an accident, and the fire carried off Mistress Mathilde too, and the baby Charles, and tell that Seraphin came to save them from the flames, and tell them that I too was caught in the fire when the house burned down! And if you tell them otherwise, then know that they will take reprisals against you, cruel reprisals. Remember this, house slaves!"

And then I went back into the burning house, I am Adelaide Beaulieu, a house slave on the Bassanville Plantation, Red Hill, Martinique, killed there, by accident, in a fire, at the age of twenty-eight, leaving behind me in this world of hatred, poverty and pain eight children, two sisters and my mother, all that was now long ago, a long long time, and so little...

IV

Mory Haidara, a noble of the Mali Empire, an Initiate, a power in the Council of Wise Men, a Master Blacksmith, returns to us to tell us of the downfall, betrayal, of his voyage, and that of his people, into the inferno.

MORY HAIDARA: I was playing with my children in front of the hut, my young brother Bokar was there too... I am Mory Haidara, Master Blacksmith, of the caste of the Initiates and Wise Men of the Mali Empire, a Master of Iron, holder of the secrets of our deceased ancestors who were expelled from the banks of the Nile more than three thousand years ago, descendant of those who fled the occupied cities, who abandoned temples and palaces to the pillagers, our pyramids, our dead, leaving behind much of the knowledge we had inscribed, burnt away from the papyrus, from our memories.

For long years then our ancestors lived as naked wanderers, as an ignorant tribe howling in the night, prowling the forest, fleeing their past glory—our great Black Egyptian civilization, the mother of all those that came after, of the white civilizations that would learn to despise and hate, and forget the black.

Their mother had been black, she is dead, and they know it but deny it, they refuse to acknowledge it. The Black Egypt of Memphis is dead, dead with Narmer Pharaoh, its First Master, the Lord who, dying, dreamed he saw his children wandering naked and bereft and illiterate, bearing with them their great tablets inscribed with the secrets of the universe to be used as pillows, until, powerful but diminished, they reached Songhai, here in our Mali Empire.

I am Mory Haidara, Master Blacksmith, of the caste of the Initiates, Master of Iron, Conscience of the Empire. With my peers we arrested Lord Sangare, master of all the counties of the Kingdom of Mali, we commanded him—this man without honor—to yield up his powers, to abdicate and lay down his arms and his armor, to give over his crown. The Council of Wise Men unmasked his corruption and evil deeds, they cast him down. And our tradition ordains that the Council of Wise Men can select as Lord and Master over us and Ruler of our Empire any Tchonde, even an ignorant man, but a man who is good, intelligent, magnanimous, and that is what we thought we were doing twenty moons ago when we chose Sangare, the bastard hyena, the stinking jackal!

Since the fall of Memphis ours has been a secret knowledge, but filthy hands have sullied it, deformed it, failed to transmit it, I cry out in the desert to warn that our language is vanishing, changing, disappearing, we will perish, but my cry no longer goes forth... The mind remains closed, our tongue is veiled.

Before Sangare we had always chosen a good Tchonde, our fault is a heavy one, the misfortune lies heavy on my people, the pervert in power now stands revealed, we had not seen it in his face, despite his trials, it is our unhappy choice, the fine gazelle has become a sly hyena, stinking and deadly, clever, the fault is ours, his eyes escaped us but not our Knowledge, our weakness.

Sylla Sidebe said as much, almost in passing, "He should have, but it is too late..." It was written in the Books: "You, sons of Narmer, descendants of the Light, the Book, the Knowledge, will know several stages in your downfall in the land of the living, you, the Heirs, the sons of Akhenaton, will know many levels of abasement, of servitude, of ruin, of shameful sufferings, down to the nethermost depths, hoping each one will be the last. Thus, for you, Black Africans, at your deaths and only then, so strangely is it written, will you return to the Glory of God and Men, only then in the knowledge of your fall will you return strengthened, in the knowledge of your fall, Men of Africa, children of Amenophis, of the African Master Menes, Black father of the Greeks, and not before! In the rediscovered memory of your place, of what Man owes you. Returned with dignity into living History. After the fall of Memphis your names, your goods, your knowledge, all were scattered, gathered up by the Barbarians who were to steal even your memory, your being, your History, violating your women, slaying your children."

We overthrew Sangare the Felon, we cast him from the Knighthood, but the Just, all the Wise Men were arrested and taken prisoner, for men knew we possessed the strength, the secrets, no one could kill us, and the men of Sangare the Hyena feared us.

Tieba spoke the Words, and our doom was sealed, it was fated to be, the Blacksmiths had erred, the fall would be severe. Always you will fall and fall again, forever and ever, for thus it is written, you will never know the depth of your torments surrounded by your demons, but in death amid the living.

They could not kill us, this they knew, and thus they sold us unto the white barbarians, men white as sour milk, men who prowled our coasts like vultures. With the exiled Just, all the knowledge, all the powers, all the science and secrets, all was given over by the Tchonde and cast into the flames, into the jaws of the vampires, and our people were bound over to ignorance, forgotten, to the darkness.

With the Wise Men they erased our four-fold thousand-year knowledge, they cast out our values, we fell ever farther from the light down into the depths where no light can be, exiles from the light we had once made burn so bright.

I was taken up into the slavers' vessel in chains, chained as we would never have chained a wild beast, a dog. With my own people, down in the hold, I tried to see... On other vessels others of the Just, less curious, had recourse to secret charms, the ships caught fire, fires the Tchonde found mysterious, fires beyond the understanding of the ignorant, and they went down, they sank full laden with Africans and crews, they sank to the bottom of the seas, but I was curious, I tried to see where the mealy-colored Barbarians would take us, to what hells, to what depths History was still going to reduce us, and I saw...I saw...horrors that no man not of my people has ever seen, I cannot speak the horror, I cannot tell it...too much horror for words...true horror cannot be spoken in the Mali tongue, the African tongue, the tongue of Man.

But I will say this to you: I stood in the marketplaces of their cities, naked to the wind as an animal, chained and muzzled, enslaved, and I saw them standing there around, red-faced, obscene, sweating and stinking, ignorant and filthy, I heard them shouting, and they felt of my body as one feels a side of beef... A sweaty fat man with a threatening gaze, bought me, and I went, I wanted to see to what limits History would force my people who were cast ever lower with each turn of fate, now surrounded by devils who churned around us as we stood, in our death.

And we came away from the slave market on foot, Africans in chains, and I saw children being dragged along like sacks of trash, and I watched them die. Seven days of march without food, with little to drink, women, children and men falling by the way, and my anger began to well from deep within me like a volcano, silently, and I walked on, for I wanted to see the creature's lair if I could, even if it meant entering within his walls, into his house, and I walked on, waiting...without dying, above the volcano, saying nothing, trying not to be, concealing my fear, my tears, my sorrow and my pain, my fatigue, my hatred, my fettered people falling all about me, their eyes cast ever lower and lower down into death, disappearing beneath the lash, undone by fear, by slavery, by shame. They stopped to get rid of the bodies and I closed my eyes, I saw Damba... The hyena-colored men tore a little girl of five from her mother's arms, for a whole hour the rat-faced men raped her as her mother screamed, her sisters screamed, before our very eyes, chained, the Gods looked down... They left the child for dead in the bushes and we set forth once more.

And when we reached the beast's lair, the "Master's House," that was what they called it, I was still standing... The first night we all slept, we slaves, chained together in the stable on a floor thick with filth, among the pigs and mules, the horses, the chickens and the donkeys, we all slept there together, broken, and I looked and saw the creature, the master of that place, with his protruding gut, his red cheeks, his snorting snores, lying unbuttoned on his unmade bed surrounded by naked young slave girls, eleven, twelve years old, torn and soiled, one crying in a corner. In another room lay the creature's wife, wrapped in her laces, skinny and bitter, and at the foot of her bed a house slave lay on the floor, and they were both asleep. And in the next room the creature's children slept as well. And there were other rooms too, rooms filled with relatives, friends, the males provided with slave women for their pleasure...so many of our women, doled out like slaves to these evil men.

And the volcano rumbled deep within me, more violently now, with terrible hunger and with no way to calm it, to stop it, the tragedy had to be buried deep, purified. I was carried up by some devastating and final force, a force that was to put me outside the law, that was to bring me to my death. And there came a boy, from his posture I could tell he was a youth of our Empire, and he was now a slave to these creatures and I recognized him: You are Pangale Keita, son of the Blacksmith Modibo Ba Keita, grandson of the great Diara Keita, and I am Mory Haidara, Master Blacksmith, member of the Council of the Just, and I am to perish, child, in this land of our desolation, there are many evils to come before the great Encounter, and I am come to tell you, child, that I was awaiting your arrival, I brought you here, we have recognized each other.

You, child, you who are left alive, do not forget to tell your children, that they may tell their children, and so on to the end of time, that they may know that in the first centuries the Great Ancient Egypt was Black, the most brilliant centuries of Mankind, tell it to your children, Pangale Keita, you who have become Edward George Jackson, tell them that Ancient Egypt, the mother of the white European civilizations, was Black, writings, sciences, mathematics, astronomy, that it was with us that all those things first shone before men, that so great was our knowledge that these greenish barbarians cannot begin to know it, only their Wise Men can know it! Since the fall of Memphis we have been spiralling down and the usurpers are everywhere, the African is still falling... So run, child, I will watch over you, and speak, as an old man speaks, to your descendants. Speak to our dispossessed and keep alive this memory of our knowledge, our existence, that we may live again after our earthly death, keep lit this flame. In you, Keita, we will live on, you will live on in this world, you and yours, unknown, for they will not find you, and in our next life we must shine bright in the shadows, the thread of our posterity must be held strongly... You will hold it as we hold the knowledge of our death. For they must not forget the barbarians' usurpation, the theft of history, the oblivion, this oblivion that kills men more surely than the worst of wars.

Now the child has gone, quietly, silently, without taking leave, solemnly, for this child was sent, it is Keita, chosen by the great Diara, his grandfather, even before the birth of his father, to perform this task... So I released my revolt and my hatred, and they emerged, they sprang out stronger than my life, and I gave a muffled cry, I summoned up the Gods, I uttered words that should not be spoken, I cursed the place, the grass, the beasts, the family, the house, I cursed their ancestors perished in other lives, I cursed them for all the other lives, I cursed and cursed, those lost souls will never rise again. I sinned in the wave and the storm...and when I opened my eyes again all around me was dead, all had burned, here the grass will never grow again, the earth will lie cursed for many moons... And when the men came everything was cinder and death, skeletons all consumed, and all was ashes, all had returned to dust as my revolt, my hatred, had ordained, all had burned as normal fire never could have burned.

And I too was there, I too was dead, and only my body had not been touched by the flames, the living came to find my flesh intact, they stood uncertain, frightened, they drew back and stood aside, they looked down upon me... I saw young Pangele standing in that murmuring crowd, standing silent amid the excited, fearful whispers, saw him looking seriously at me. He knew...

And I looked at the new nightmare world for my people, theirs until the Encounter, as it is written. Oh Son of Narmer, Son of the Master Scientists of Memphis, my death is written in our fall. The Sangare will continue to pillage for a time, the barbarians will continue to sell them our Africa to despoil, to burn, to hack apart, to create the last great desert of sand where only the shadows of my people's ghosts will walk. And on a continent ravaged by the deaths of plant, of beast, of Man, only the barbarians from the North will utter the lies, the duplicity, the barbarians come here to grow rich, to revel.

Soon, dead Africa, deserted Africa, continent of the moon...the few Black survivors, scattered, caught up in another History, other lies, will no longer understand.

~

Bernard-Marie Koltès

Night Just Before the Forest

Translated from the French by
Timothy Johns

UBU REPERTORY THEATER PUBLICATIONS
NEW YORK

Bernard-Marie Koltès was born in Metz in 1948 and died in Paris in 1989. His plays have been performed in Europe, Scandinavia, Australia and the U.S. Koltès studied at the Théâtre National de Strasbourg from 1970 to 1977, where he directed student productions of his own plays—*Les Amertumes* (1970) adapted from Gorky's *Childhood, La Marche* (1970) inspired by the *Song of Songs, Procès ivre* (1971) inspired by *Crime and Punishment,* and two plays later broadcast on French radio, *L'Héritage* (1972) and *Des Voix sourdes* (1974). With *Night Just Before the Forest* (1977) he returned to writing after a three-year interval. First produced at the 1977 Avignon festival, it was later performed in Paris (1981) and received first prize at the 1981 Fringe Festival in Edinburgh. Timothy Johns' English translation of the play had its first reading in the U.S. by Gilbert Price at Ubu Repertory Theater in 1983. Koltès travelled frequently throughout his life and often lived in foreign countries for several months at a time. In 1979, he settled for six months in Guatemala where he wrote *Struggle of the Dogs and the Black,* inspired by his first trip to Africa. The play was given its world premiere in 1982, under the title of *Come Dog, Come Night* in an Ubu Repertory Theater–La Mama E.T.C. co-production, directed by Françoise Kourilsky. The translation was by Matthew Ward. The first French production, in 1983, was directed by Patrice Chéreau who also directed the premieres of Koltès' *Quai ouest* (1986), *Dans la solitude des champs de coton* (1987), and *Retour au désert* (1988). Koltès' last play, *Roberto Zucco,* was written in 1988 and premiered two years later in German under the direction of Peter Stein at the Schaubühne in Berlin. It has since been produced in Paris (1991) and New York (1995). Koltès' adaptation of Athol Fugard's *The Blood Knot* was produced at the 1982 Avignon Festival and his translation of *A Winter's Tale* was produced in Paris in 1988. He also wrote one novel, *La Fuite à cheval très loin dans la ville,* in 1976. It was published in 1984 by Editions de Minuit, his French publisher. *Night Just Before the Forest* and *Struggle of the Dogs and the Black* have been published in one volume by Ubu Repertory Theater Publications, in 1983. Timothy Johns has revised his translation of *Night Just Before the Forest* for this anthology.

Timothy Johns's translations of Jean-Louis Bourdon's *Jock,* Denise Bonal's *Family Portrait* and *A Picture Perfect Sky,* Tchicaya u' Tam'Si's *The Glorious Destiny of Marshal Nnikon Nniku* and Jean-Paul Wenzel's *Vater Land, the Country of our Fathers* have all been published by Ubu Repertory Theater Publications.

TRANSLATOR'S NOTE

It was Rudi and Italian wine that started it. So long ago now it seems only last week, Rudi Laurent, Parisian actor/director in New York with a lot of time on his hands, came around to me with a pile of pages and said, read it: it's a great piece, if you like it and want to, I'll help and bring you two bottles of Italian red each session, once a week.

Rudi knew me. Fact is, as it turned out, the pages he gave me, this "play," this long, twisted, difficult, breathless and wrenching note from the underground, made by one Bernard-Marie Koltès, had me in its grip from the very first phrase. I couldn't wait to get started. Whatever this voice was, and it certainly was strange, it also rang very familiar. Yet there was so much I didn't understand about the time and the place and the language! So of course I agreed, and once a week, whether with this or that Barolo, Chianti or Montepulciano d'Abruzzo, or wines whose names have long since evaporated into the general oblivion, Rudi and I would get together and discover the true meaning of "pouring over a text." We worked well together, we tried to serve Bernard, and laughed a lot doing it.

Later on, when, to my complete surprise, an organization known as Ubu Repertory Theater and its director, Françoise Kourilsky, showed an interest in the translation and wanted to publish it, Rudi refused any money or even any acknowledgement in its preparation. I am here to tell you today that he was the instigator and the driving force behind it.

Always in the background, too, was an image of the invisible creator of this ferocious, haunting voice; he must, I thought, look a lot like the wild and whirling words his character talked. I pictured a sallow, brooding, hollow-cheeked sort, a cross between Rasputin and Raskolnikov, and I confess that when the

NIGHT JUST BEFORE THE FOREST

shy, ruddy, smiling boy (there is no other word for Bernard) was introduced to me in New York by Rudi, I couldn't help but feel astonishment at the thought that this gentle, modest soul created *La Nuit juste avant les forêts*. I still can't. Bernard's later meteoric success didn't surprise me at all; what never ceases to amaze me is the fact that this tender-hearted, essentially friendly man, this shy guy in jeans and sneakers who put you so immediately at ease, had the power to write so disturbingly.

So in this brief little space, let me propose a toast to these two: Bernard-Marie Koltès and Rudi Laurent. Bernard, if you were still alive, I know you'd be blushing and smiling. And Rudi, wherever you are, I know you're doing beautifully.

Shall we make it a Barolo?

TIMOTHY JOHNS

You were turning the corner when I saw you, it's pouring rain, my hair and clothes are sopping wet which doesn't make it any easier but I got up the nerve anyway and now that we're here I don't even want to look at myself, I really ought to go dry off, go back downstairs and spruce up a bit, my hair at least dry it out so I don't get sick, while ago I did go down just to see if I could, but down there is where the assholes all hang out, and the whole time you're trying to dry your hair they lurk around in packs eyeing you behind your back, so I came up after only a pee with my clothes still sopping wet, and it'll stay like this 'til we find a room somewhere, once we're settled somewhere I can take 'em all off, which is why I'm looking for a room, 'cause see, my room there's no way I can go back there, not for the rest of the night at least, which is why you, when I saw you turning the corner back there I ran and I thought to myself, there's really nothing easier to find than a room for the night, not if you really want one, not if you get up the nerve to ask for it, in spite of your wet clothes and soaked hair, in spite of the rain, which leaves me limp when I look in a mirror, but even if you don't want to it's hard not to look at yourself with all these mirrors around here in the bars and hotels, so many to keep behind your back, like right now when it's you they're watching, personally I keep 'em in back of me, even at home, even if there's a lot of them, like practically everywhere around here, even in the hotels where there are thousands of mirrors looking at you that you gotta watch out for, 'cause personally I've almost always lived in hotels, and said home while ago just out of habit, what it is really is a hotel room, and except for tonight when I just can't do it, that's what home is, and when I check into a hotel room, it's such an old routine of mine that in a minute I can turn it into my own home with just a few little touches, make it look like I've always lived there, make it look like the usual old room I always live in with all my usual habits, with the mirrors all hidden and bare to the bone, to the point that if anybody ever took a notion to make me live in a real room in a real house, or gave me one of those apartments like the kind real families live in, as soon as I walked in I'd turn it into a hotel room, just by living there, just out of habit, or even if they gave me one of those little fairy-tale cottages deep inside a forest, with huge wooden beams and a great big fireplace, huge pieces of furniture you've never seen the likes of and thousands of years old, as soon as I stepped in, with just a few touches and in a minute I'd have you something that looked a lot like a hotel room, a place I'd feel at home in, over here I'd hide the fireplace behind a big stack of furniture, over there I'd simply wave away those big wooden beams, I'd change everything around, dump out all the old fairy-tale stuff you never see anywhere else, and the smells, those special family smells, and the old stone and the old dark wood, and the thousands of years of age that mock you and make you feel like a stranger, that never let you feel completely at home, I'd throw it all out and all the old stuff with it, that's the way I am, I don't like stuff that reminds you you're a stranger, even though to a certain extent I guess that's what I am, it's pretty obvious I'm not altogether from around here, definitely obvious to those assholes downstairs ganged up behind my back after I'd peed and was washing my weenie, makes you realize just how fucking dumb the French really are, absolutely no imagination, just because they've never seen anybody wash his weenie before, for us it's an old custom my own father taught me, back home we always did it, and I still do it every time after I pee, so while I was downstairs washing my weenie as usual and felt all the assholes lurking around behind my back, I just played like I couldn't understand, just like the total foreigner who couldn't possibly understand a word of their asshole French, so while I was washing it I could hear: "hey what's this weirdo doin', anyway?"—"he's giving his weenie a drink, stupid"—"that's bullshit, giving his weenie a drink!"—just like I couldn't understand a word they were saying, and I calmly keep giving it a drink while the pack of French assholes behind me starts asking each other, right up in front of the sink "yeah, so tell me how's a weenie drink, huh?" "how's a weenie s'posed to get thirsty anyways?"— so then when I finished, I made my way back through the pack, still like the total foreigner who didn't understand a word of what they were saying, which is easy enough for me since I'm not from here anyway, not altogether, which is pretty obvious since even those totally unimaginative French assholes could see it, but still, in spite of all that, I ran after you as soon as I saw you turning the corner, in spite of all the assholes out in the streets, in the bars, in the basements of bars, here, there, all around us, in spite of the rain and my rain-soaked clothes, I ran after you not just for the sake of the room, not even for that part of the night I need a room for, but I ran and ran and ran so that this once, once I've turned the corner, I don't just find myself all alone in a street without you, that this once I don't just find the rain and the rain and the rain, so that just this once, I find you around the corner, and I get up the nerve to say: "brother!", I get up the nerve to take you by the arm: "brother!", I get up the nerve to go up to you and say "got a light brother?" it won't cost you a thing brother, fuck this god-damned rain, fuck the god-damned wind, and god damn this street corner, sure isn't a night to be walking around in for either one of us you know, fact is it wasn't so much 'cause I wanted a smoke that I said "got a light brother," I don't even have a cigarette, no, what I meant to say instead was: fuck this god-damn corner, brother, and to hell with this routine of walk-ing around out here (what a way to come on to somebody!), and you too, here you are walking around out here with your clothes sopping wet, catching your death maybe of god knows what kinds of diseases, no I'm not asking for a cigarette either, brother, I don't even smoke, won't cost you a thing, not even a light or a cigarette, for damn sure not any money (otherwise you'd drop me on the spot), actually I've got a bit of cash to spare tonight, fact is I've got enough to buy us a coffee, brother, I'd rather buy you a coffee than walk around here in this weird light, so see my way of coming on to you isn't gonna cost you a thing, I may have my way of coming on to people, but it never costs them a thing in the end (and I'm not talking about a room, brother, a room for the night, 'cause that's when the nice guys freeze up and you'd drop me on the spot, no, no, we're not even talking about a room brother), but it's this plan of mine I've got to tell you about—come on, if we stick around out here we'll catch our death for sure—no money, out of work, that doesn't help either (not that I'm really looking anymore, but that's beside the point) it's just that this plan I have to tell you about, see, you and me, wandering around here in this weird town stone broke (wait I'm gonna buy you a coffee man, really, I've got enough, I'm not goin' back on my word), you can tell right off we're not weighed down in this shit by tons of money! so like I say, I've got this plan, brother, for people like you and me who got no job, got no money, not that I'm really looking anymore—see what I mean is that people like us, working outdoors, without a penny in our pockets, we don't really weigh too much, see, and we could easily get swept up and blown away by just one tiny little gust of wind, they'd practically have to strap us down on a scaffolding, one little gust of wind and we'd take off light as a feather—and hey, you see me working in a factory? no way! it's sorta hard to explain and even for me it's not that easy to understand all of it without getting mixed up, but what I meant to say is this, see, my plan, it's not some religion, not some bullshit you can just put any old way regardless and it doesn't make any difference, it's not like politics, for sure not some party or anything like that, like the unions who know it all and have seen it all and don't miss a thing (no room for any of that in my plan), all of that's got nothing to do with it, no, my plan's nothing of the sort, believe you me: it's for our own self-defense, it's purely defensive, 'cause that's what we really need, isn't it, to defend ourselves? I know you're thinking, speak for yourself buddy, but let me tell you: o.k. maybe it was me who came on to you first, maybe I am the one who needs a room for the night (no, no brother I didn't say I really needed one), and so maybe I did say: "got a light brother?" but it's not always the one who makes the first move who's the weakest, you know, and I noticed right away you don't seem all that strong, walking around back there dripping wet, not too strong at all, whereas me, in spite of it all, I do have some resources, like I have the ability to spot the weak ones right away, see, just by a little glance, just from the way they move, 'specially from that tense little way of walking, nervous like you, with the nervous back and that nervous way the shoulders roll, something about that way of moving which never fools me, even when they roll and strut around like big tough guys, but tough guys with a case of nerves, you know? like those street kids hanging out, but straight from their mother's lap, with those torsos of theirs they roll and flex like this like it was nothing out there in the rain, 'cause me I can see right away the nervousness there, they can't hide it from me, see, 'cause all those nerves, now, that comes from the mother, straight from the mother, and those kids, whatever else they can do, they can't hide their mother, while with me now it's more in the muscle and the blood and flesh and bone, everything that comes from the father, nerves never bug me, 'cause my father he was just the opposite, a tough son-of-a-bitch, not exactly the kind of guy who has a nervous breakdown from over-thinking, nothing bugged him, a man all bone and muscle and blood, you might've called him the executioner, for that matter you might even call me the executioner, which is why politics, parties, the unions, the way they are today, and the cops, the military, all of which are political, that shit's not what I'm looking for, all that shit's too tangled up in the head and believe me with that head they'll stick you right in a factory, and me in a factory? no way! but they still end up sticking you in a factory, whereas the plan I was telling you about, it's a union on an international scale— that's very important, on an international scale!—(I'll explain it, really, it's just not that easy to follow), but no politics, only self-defense, and personally I'm made for defense, so me I'll completely devote myself to that, I'll be the executioner in my international union, defending the kids who aren't so tough, those mothers' boys out all night walking around like tough guys with a case of nerves, rolling and strutting around all alone, risking god-knows-what sorts of diseases—and of course that's where I see the uselessness of the mother, look at how useless your mother is: she gives you a nervous system and later she drops you out on a street corner out in some bitch of a storm, weak and too trusting, 'cause I see all too clearly that you're too trusting as little and nervous as you are, you're much too trusting, and don't think for a minute that the bastards aren't out there and that they aren't watching you, me I know damned well we brush by them in the street, and just while ago I screwed up and damn near really got fucked over, I'm just like you, too trusting, yeah, but now I see them everywhere, they're around here all right, the worst sons-of-bitches you can imagine, the bastards who make us live like this, me I used to think they were invisible, hidden away up there somewhere above the bosses, above the government, way up there above it all, bastards with faces like killers and rapists and plan-perverters, not with real faces like yours and mine, but totally anonymous: a gang of con-artists, cushy crooks and scot-free perverts, cold, calculating technicians, a little gang of technical bastards who orders you: "to the factory and keep quiet!" (hey, me in a factory? no way!), "to the factory and shut your traps" (and suppose I open my trap?), "to the factory, and shut the fuck up we've got the last word" and they do have the last word, that little cabal of fuckers who orders us around from up there, plotting and calculating among themselves, technicians on an international scale, an international scale! now me and my plan, it's for a union on an international scale, and I'm gonna tell you all about it, but see now that we're already fucked it's either the factory or growing light as a feather like you and me and getting blown away by the slightest little breeze, 'cause what else

can we do, you and me, when they run the government, the
police, the military, the bosses, the streets, the neighborhoods,
the subways, the light, and when if they wanted to from up there
they could have us completely wiped out, what could I do against
all that without my union plan? you, you're too trusting, like
me a while ago, but they're out there all right and they're looking for us, they've come down among us and I nearly got
badly fucked over, 'cause some of the worst bastards you can
imagine take on the weirdest shapes and the strangest ways, oh
sure if they came down here right away, so we could see it on
their faces, if we could see right away who we had to deal with,
then we could really put up a fight, but what they do instead
is, they rub up against us with their irresistible looks so that of
course we lose control of ourselves and, in total trust, get our
asses kicked by the worst kinds of bitches—but how can you
tell? me I couldn't; if it had been all make-believe, I would've
imagined her exactly as she was, just like when I first saw her
and went up to her, small and delicate, a full blonde with
highlights in her curls, only not too curly and not too blonde,
just enough to make it believable, to make it impossible not to
run after her, so when I went up to her and said, 'scuse me sister, you wouldn't have a light would you, her eyes looking up
at me like only in make-believe, shining just like I would've
imagined them, like in some daydream on an evening when
everything's deserted and there's nothing happening, but there
are other evenings, when in spite of the rain, in spite of this
filthy light and the night itself which gets in the way of everything, there are evenings when girls are walking around—not
just one every now and then, but lots of them, one after the
other more and more beautiful, enough to drive you crazy, drive
you crazier and crazier hour after hour, one hour to the next
girls more and more incredible until you think it's never going
to stop, and it keeps growing and growing and you start feeling so high you can't think anymore with all these girls parading past! and just when you think it can't get any better, and

you can't get any crazier from staring at them, one of them lands right in front of you, one just like her, and you drop everything and run after her, just like you're supposed to, in spite of your empty pockets and the rain which leave you completely helpless, but this one you've got to go after, go up to her, what with her hair and her eyes peering up at you, looking so fragile and not too curly: sister! sister! and it's precisely that sister, sister!—that they've been waiting for, and it's right then and there that you get fucked over like the dumbest asshole on the block; oh if I'd have known that she was on the other side, that she was a bitch—"come on along with me tonight, pretty boy, we're gonna hunt some sand-niggers"—if she had kept her mouth shut I never would've learned just what kind of crap a mouth like hers could spit out, (used to be, when I was still working, I thought everyone, including the girls out at night, that everyone was the same deep down, and that you could talk to them, just a question of getting up the nerve, everyone that is except the little gang of bastards with killer faces, but now I believe the whole world has gone over to the other side, and never again will I ever run after one of those girls who drive you crazy, and never ever will I go crazy again), she, she didn't recognize me, on account of the light which made us look so much alike "we'll go hunt some sand-niggers, pretty boy, and then you'll come home with me!"—she says this right up close in that weird cafe she'd taken me to (holding me by the hand, clinging to me, all hot to spend the night with me, to get me back to her room, and oh she wanted me no doubt about it, before I got mad at hearing the bitch's bullshit and she got mad at what I said oh we wanted each other all right), but what do you know? she didn't realize who I was—the wave of the future, that's us, she tells me, and you ought to join up—well I might have done it with all those mind-boggling looks she was giving me, but the worst kind of international and technical bitchiness takes on forms exactly like that, they've made everybody go over to the other side, even those incredible women who'd drive you completely wild if only they didn't talk, but her, I was afraid of what she was saying and the way she said it and the fact that I couldn't keep from listening, but she still didn't recognize me in that weird cafe—"come on along with me, pretty boy"—and I might well have done it like the dumbest asshole on the block, if there hadn't slipped out of my mouth, just in time (and even louder than I'd intended), who I was: sister, this is who I am: a stranger, international union, and so on, and now if you don't shut your mouth I am going to bash it in for you—and I would've too, if only all those friends of hers hadn't been around, those Saturday night sand-nigger-hunters, that brigade of pretty-boys armed to the teeth, and me there all alone and a stranger against all of them, what had I gotten myself into like some poor dumb fuck? and with that light there that had kept me in the dark, but just what if, before all that happened to come out of my mouth, forced out just in time, what if she'd started singing instead? what if, instead of spitting out all that crap (since she trusted me) she had sung it to me? she could've sung anything to me, I'd've been help-less and agreed to anything, I'd have kept my identity secret, I'd've joined anything, young wavers-of-the-future, fascists, roy-alists, right-wingers, racists, organized fuckers and international cartels of con-men, I'd've said whatever she wanted, hunted whatever she asked, and all because she was so unbelievably beautiful, and all because of what she had promised us after that hunt, because of the fact that she made me drop every-thing and run after her, and that if she had sung, she proba-bly would have sung like an angel, what could I have done? stop up my ears? and if she'd have put her lips up close to my ear, what could I have done? run away? if she had placed her hand on my thigh, what could I do then, huh? chop it off? chop off my own weenie? 'cause that's where they get you, like the dumb-est ass on the block, so what you have to do now is tie it down hard, deprive yourself even of that and be damned sure you don't get fucked over! strangers like us, brother, we've got to deprive ourselves of everything and tie it down tight; the main thing about my union plan, see, is once and for all to stop getting hard-ons, as long as everything's controlled by the secret little cabal that owns the ministers, the cops, the army, the jobs, all the way down to the little bitches with curly blond hair who look so incredibly fragile and yet who've gone over to the other side just like everyone else, stop getting hard-ons, stop getting off, hold yourself down at all costs, 'cause that's what they're aiming for and that's where they fuck you, with all our might and with all our means hold it down tight until we've won, until my international union plan finally wins out, and then, it'll all be ours, the cafes, the streets, the bitches, the pretty-boys and their weapons, the whole heaven and earth, and then it's gonna be the sand-niggers' time to get off, boy, it'll be our turn, and myself as executioner, made of muscle and blood and bone, myself deprived for so long, for so long forced to hold myself in, it's gonna be my turn then to kick some ass, brother, and that's one pleasure I am not going to deprive myself of, I'll hunt 'em down everywhere, where are they now the fuckers who used to spit on me? and I'll find them all, because that is going to be the moment when there's no longer any holding back, brothers: skin 'em alive, get all the hard-ons you can and get off on it, come as much as you can, and all the come you've held in for so long come all over their faces, drown those killer faces and those lovely faces of the elite who got off on each other at our expense for so long—but I'll say this as well: if you happen to meet somewhere, someone still walking around and around with his shoulders loose like a real tough guy, one of those nervous little cases straight from his mother, left there defenseless on a street corner for no reason, rolling and strutting about like some tough guy, then let him alone, don't hit him, don't touch him, he's still a kid and we have to defend him—and so there it is, you have my plan, and let me tell you it won't be long either, even if right now we are practically broke, without work, even if I don't have a room to sleep in for the night, and you, for the moment, you've got to be on your guard, and if somebody asks you: who's that stranger with you? who's that stranger with you? you answer: I don't know, I don't know, and if they insist, you say: I hardly know him, he's just some guy who came up to me in the street as I was turning the corner back there, asking me for a room to spend the night in, or not even the whole night, never saw him before, because you know I noticed from far away that you were just a child, kind of a kid dumped on a street corner, liable to get blown away by the tiniest little gust of wind, and whenever I run after you, once, twice, three times, there's never anything there but an empty street and the rain, but this time, I decided not to lose out anymore, I left nothing to chance, this time I was ready; I made sure the assholes weren't in my way, I agreed with them, pretended to listen to their bullshit and agreed with all of it, all that bullshit they rattle on about outside every night, in spite of this goddamn rain and sad light, and all that's like some exotic flock of birds that only exists in the minds of assholes, and if you want to agree with them all, you give your opinion and make up a bunch of colorful details, which is what I was doing, made up a bunch of colors and disguised the fact that I was a stranger while I pronounced my opinion on all the general topics, all the particular topics, fashion, politics and so on, I controlled myself very well, kept the wind to my back, kept my back turned to the wind so I wouldn't be caught completely helpless when I finally took off after you, and there I was saying to myself there's nothing easier than feeling which way the wind is blowing, or getting them on your side so they don't get in the way—and nothing could give me away, my foreign weenie I kept well hidden and under control, my hand on my zipper, I held back the need to pee and so give myself away by carelessly giving it a drink, 'cause there they really would've recognized me, no doubt about it, recognized me as a stranger there among them, but for the moment I was managing quite well, in that weird light which makes us indistinguishable, makes out of all those gabby cafe-and-street creeps people with the same looks and the same concerns and disguises the guy whose mind is somewhere else, a stranger to all of them, with my furtive glance searching beyond them, I'd keep my back turned like theirs into the wind, smiling and agreeing, already half-drunk with made-up concerns, and thinking: mine is elsewhere and I've got to hide it, and when I saw you, I ran and ran and ran and no one got in the way, I'd made sure I was on their side, I'd listened to them, hiding my difference and now my flight takes them by surprise, I'm already at the corner when they wake up and recognize me as a stranger and start tailing me with their bullshit, getting ready to take me by surprise somewhere else, like down there while ago, but already I was on my way up to you and saying: 'scuse me I noticed you turning the corner, sorry I'm half drunk and probably not at my best, but I've lost my room, I'm looking for a room just for tonight, or just for part of the night, 'cause in five minutes I won't be drunk anymore, all I ask is five minutes—so there I was saying I was drunk and asking for five minutes, half my head still stuffed with bullshit, the other half completely with you, and I could hardly get up the nerve even to look at you I was still so befuddled by fashion, politics, salaries, and so on—when I was still working, my salary seemed like some tiny exotic bird that would fly into the room and that I'd shut in, but as soon as I'd crack open the door, out it would fly away suddenly never to come back, and all that was left was to miss it forever, and now I don't work anymore—but still I hadn't gotten up the nerve to look at the guy whose arm I was holding: all I ask is five minutes, enough to sober up, then we'll sit down, I'll buy us a coffee, I'll sit him down facing me and the mirror behind my back, then forget about the rest: this god-damn rain, filthy light, the idling assholes and the depressing colors they've left in my head, I'll look at him, I'll get up the nerve in spite of my sopping wet hair and clothes that won't dry off, in spite of that I'll wait 'til I've recovered my resources—I'm looking for a room for part of the night, 'cause I can't find mine anymore: I wanted to ask you the minute I saw you on the corner, I'd never in a million years ask one of those assholes I was hanging around with, even though I don't look at all like them (which is probably obvious) but I was hanging out with them for a thousand reasons, always keeping half myself hidden in this search for a room where I wouldn't be stuck with an asshole, forced to hide the fact that I'm a stranger, forced to talk about fashion, politics, salaries, food, all those French assholes with the same faces and the same interests, talking about food even out there in the rain, keeping their backs to the wind and talking about food, and there I was nodding and agreeing, so I'd be free any minute to run and run and run, me, who doesn't even eat, who eats absolutely nothing, who gets lighter and lighter day after day, who refuses to put on weight, that way I can conduct my search in secret, beyond the gluttons who stand around in circles outside and in the cafes, I kept agreeing and nodding, getting drunk on the food they talked about, feeling the wind at my back beginning to lift me a little, and it would've carried me away if I hadn't quietly been hanging onto the fat gluttons with their lead-heavy bullshit, would've blown me away I've become so light, like those breezes which used to whisk you away around street corners when I'd see you, once, twice, three times, seeing quite clearly from a distance that you were still a kid, so I dropped everything, the wind picked me up and I started running, hardly noticing if my feet were still touching the ground, running as fast as you this time without anything in the way, and so, finally, to go up to you and say: don't take me for a queer, man, just because I run and stop you and take you by the arm and talk to you without really knowing you, although I know you well enough, man, to tell you about this thing with a woman on a bridge—which I can't keep to myself, and anyway you think a queer would get up the nerve to make a pass without all his resources, with his clothes and hair sopping wet? you see me here like this, still not quite right in the head (but that'll go away) and at first sight, I saw clearly that you're the decent sort of guy one can talk to: I don't know her real name, the one she gave me wasn't hers, so I won't mention how she looked either, the two of us will never know who we made love to all night one night out on a bridge, right in the middle of a city, there are still traces of it there in the stone: you go out for a walk, doesn't matter where, one night by chance you see a girl leaning over the water, you happen to move closer, she turns around and says: my name is mama, don't tell me yours, don't tell me yours, and you don't tell her yours, you say: where to? and she says: where do you want? why not here? so you stay there 'til it's nearly dawn and she goes away, and all night long I'm asking: who are you? where do you live? what do you do? where do you work? will we see each other again? and she says, leaning over the water: "I never leave it, I go from one bank to another, from one bridge to another, I go back up the canal and come back down to the river, I watch the barges, look at the locks, look for the bottom of the water, I sit down beside the water and lean over, me, I can't even talk except on a bridge or on a bank, and that's the only place I can really make love, anywhere else and I'm practically dead, all day long I'm bored and every night I come back to be close to the water, and we don't leave each other until daybreak"—then she goes away and I let her without even moving (at morning on the bridges, it's teeming with people and cops), I stayed on in the middle of that bridge until noon, that's not her real name and I didn't tell her mine, the two of us will never know who we made love to one night lying on the edge of the bridge (at noon, it's noisy and full of cops, you can't stay there right in the middle of a bridge without moving), so during the day I wrote all over the walls: mama I love you mama I love you on all the walls, so there'd be no way she could miss it, I'll be there on the bridge, mama, all night long, the same bridge as the other night, all day long I ran around like a madman: come back mama come back, and like a madman I'd write: mama, mama, mama, and at night I'd wait there right in the middle of the bridge, as soon as it was day I'd start again on the wall, all the walls so there'd be no way she could miss it: come back to the bridge, come back one more time, just once more, come back just for one minute so I can see you, mama, mama, but dammit man like an asshole I waited one, two, three or more nights, I ransacked every bridge, I'd run from one to another several times every night, thirty-one bridges there are not counting the canals, and during the day I'd write, I'd cover the walls completely, no way she could've missed it, but dammit man she never came, she never would come again, but I still kept on writing all over the walls, kept ransacking the bridges, all thirty-one not counting the canals, and I never found her again, leaning over the water, and now don't you know stories like that really get me down, really bewilders me when things go too far, there's this woman I know who's dead because things had gone too far, really gets me down the number of people who'd die if it were easier, the number who'd go that far if only there were some way, or if the way weren't always so scary, and then you're never sure you'll really succeed, it can take a long time, and the day they invent some god-awful way which is gentle and available for everyone, then it's gonna be a god-awful slaughter for those cases which always go too far, a god-awful slaughter for sure, like that woman who did herself in by eating dirt, she goes right down into the cemetery and starts digging right next to the graves, brings up a handful of dirt, the deepest dirt she can get to, then she swallows it—stories like that one, once you get too wrapped up in them and let yourself go, they can really drive you crazy—'cause, see the dirt in cemeteries, I mean the dirt which touches the coffins: "you, who choke the dead to death, you with your god-awful way of strangling the life out of everyone so deep down they never come back, once and for all, please, choke to death this crazy bitch that I've become!"— who was it told her that little trick would work? the crazy bitch of a whore eating dirt 'til she dies, in the middle of a grave-

yard there where I saw her plain as day—that somebody would
tell her that, that really gets me down, some other old whore
no doubt with a whole stack of recipes—a god-awful slaughter,
no fuss no bother!—but it's not everybody who can eat dirt and
if they did invent a method (say, instead of dirt, some fine light
powder which goes down nice and smooth, free of charge,
which puts you to sleep when things go too far), then the whole
world would choke the life out of itself at the tiniest setback,
'cause if you let yourself go it's the little things, the tiny little
things which end up going too far and completely bewilder
you, and yet, the one I told you about, she was a whore, I'd seen
her before one night on that street of theirs up in a fourth-floor
window, and ever since then I followed her, all the way to the
cemetery, it's hard to believe of a whore, even they are going
bonkers, a little later I'll show you that window, but personally,
these days I'm in favor of getting off my rocks and splitting: o.k.
by you? great!—splitting no fuss no bother, before the big
speeches begin, and anyway one fuck is all you need to know
all there is to know, find out all there is to find out, I could live
a hundred thousand years with a chick and not find out any
more about her at the end of three hundred thousand years
than I knew from the very first fuck, which is why I prefer it this
way: o.k. by you? okay let's go!—and split right after, knowing
what there is to know, thinking what there is to think, having
my opinion on the matter, because man, what do you think?
how can you have an opinion about somebody unless you've
fucked her? a hundred thousand years with her without fucking and you still wouldn't know a thing, except for the big
speeches which drive you up the wall, what do you find out
about her from the big speeches unless you already know
what she's like, unless you know how she moves, how she breathes,
if she talks and makes a fuss, or if she wants you very much
and doesn't say a word, holds herself back, keeps everything a
secret just for you and just for her, what can you learn about
somebody if you don't know how she breathes after she fucks,
whether she keeps her eyes shut tight or opens them up, or if

you don't listen for a long time to the noise she makes and the time she takes in between breaths, or where she lays her head and how her face looks now, and the longer she lies there breathing and you beside her listening quietly to her breathe, the more you learn about her, but the moment she sits up, opens her eyes, puts her chin in her hand, fixes you with her stare, starts breathing normally again and opens up her mouth where you can see the big speeches gathering at the exit, let me tell you I'm out the door right then and there: o.k.? o.k.!— but that night I was all alone down on the whores' street, one Friday night back when I was still working and didn't have to get up the next day, I look up and there in a fourth-floor window is the face of this whore who looks completely out of her mind—if you want to we can go back and look at it, that window I'm talking about, I'm not gonna go there by myself, personally they really get me down those whores, specially on a night like tonight, not that I'm afraid of a Friday night any more than any other night, on the contrary, now that I don't work anymore I kind of miss the way it used to be on Friday evenings and all the rest of the night when you don't have to get up the next day, when everybody's exhaustion shows in their face and nobody wants to call it quits, they all get worked up and let themselves go, mouthing off and bellowing about bashing in somebody's face, here, guys mouth off a lot about it but they take their precious time to bash it in—back home we hit 'em right off without any lip, we're not shy about it, but here, they like to give you the third degree first—whadda you want? you talkin' to me? whaddaya think you're lookin' at? what's so funny about that? you touchin' me? and it takes them about a zillion years to finish asking you if you're really touching them before they go ahead and bash in your face, personally I hit 'em right off without being shy about it, that you can be sure of, so that's where I was looking, right up at the fourth-floor window that crazy-looking whore was opening while she kept glancing back over her shoulder, she opens it very softly, disappears into the back of the apartment and then comes back, but I mean with a look on her face absolutely and totally deranged, with a big pile of clothes in her arms, later on we'll go over there and see where it was, as long as you're not afraid, no need to be afraid with me along, if they even say a word to me I clobber 'em, so then everybody in the street sees this pair of pants sailing down and landing like a sack right in the middle of the sidewalk, then a red jacket floating down softly like a parachute, then his sheer, silky underwear and shirt hanging off the lamppost, with his tie dangling down, and everybody's staring up at this whore's crazed face leaning out of the window and watching these clothes plummet to the street or dangle in the air— "and now he's naked he's completely naked!"—this guy has got himself a real wacko this time, everybody mutters to himself out there in the street, looking at the clothes on the sidewalk and the rest flapping like flags from the lamppost—hard to believe from a whore, even they're going crazy now, everybody's thinking, and they start to get a little edgy about the whores' street, where to now? they're saying to themselves, turning up their collars and edging away—where to now? where now? they're wondering, as if, from way up there somewhere, somebody had drawn up a map of special zones where they're supposed to stay all week long until the doors open up every Friday night into the whores' street and so on, and if not—where to?— and there's no other alternative, since I stopped working, personally I've been able to figure out the entire series of zones which the bastards have mapped out for us, which they shut us up in with a flick of their pens, work zones for all week, zones for cars and zones for cruising, zones for women and zones for men, zones for queers, zones for sadness, zones for gabbing, zones for sorrow, and then the zones for Friday night, the Friday night zone I lost ever since I got it all mixed up, the one I want to find again I felt so good there, I can't tell you how good, but since then I don't work anymore and everything on the bastards' maps is all mixed up, night after night I've been looking for wherever it was on those Friday nights when I felt so good, with no work the next day when I fucked on a bridge and hung out in strange neighborhoods, so lonely I couldn't even tell you, come on along we'll find it again, no need to be afraid, I'm not afraid to fight and I pop 'em right away, and on a Friday night with their big mouths and their exhaustion, those guys who get all worked up are scareder than we are, they shoot off at the mouth out of fear, they get into fights out of fear, they bash your face in with more fear in their fists than in ours, in their fists, their legs, their mouths, fear that somebody's looking at them, fear that nobody's looking at them, fear that somebody's laughing at them, fear that nobody's thinking about them, fear of the other kids who look like them too much, and even more fear of the ones who don't look like them at all, come on I'll show you the window where that whore watched the clothes dangling, then this guy in a fury, with his hair standing on end, walking as fast as he can, and behind him the whore's voice:—"he's naked under the overcoat! stark naked under his coat!"—and the guy picks up his jacket, his pants, looks up at his shirt in a rage and at his tie and underwear waving like banners on top of the lamppost, and everybody turns up his collar and wonders:—where to? where to now?—the whore chases after the guy like a raving lunatic, she herself is half naked, you see the guy get into his car and start the engine, the whore hangs on to the door-handle and climbs up on the hood—"don't let him go! don't let him go!"—and this guy in a rage starts up the engine anyway, while everyone else starts edging away glancing back over their shoulders and wondering where to go, where to go to now; good lord now it's even the whores, it's unbelievable, and then she lets herself tumble off the hood and stretches out right in front of the wheels, and this guy, in a rage, suddenly has to stop, he starts honking away like crazy but the whore keeps lying there in front of the car, and everybody edges away turning up their collars—"help! help! don't let him go away!"—and then everyone's gone except for a few old whores, no doubt it was one of them who gave her that recipe: you go into the cemetery where the dirt there will choke to death anybody who's going crazy—who was it who gave her the tip? and now it really gets me down to go back there to that street alone, because I always ask:—you know that whore who died from eating dirt?—and they treat me like some screwball—you know that whore from the fourth floor? then they call in their pimps to get rid of me, and yet I saw her myself there, dead in the cemetery, and now the thought of it, man, just the thought of it makes me sick, makes me want to drink (if it weren't for this problem of money), to get out of here (if only we knew where to go), be in a room somewhere, pal, where I could talk, here I don't seem to be able to say what I have to tell you, it's got to be somewhere else, somewhere with nobody around, no more of these money problems, no more of this god-damned rain, somewhere comfortable, like on the grass some place where we could sit down, some place like that where you wouldn't have to move anymore, with plenty of time ahead of you, somewhere in the shade of a tree, where I'll be able to say: I'm home, I feel fine here, I'm gonna lie down now, so long—but that, my friend, just isn't possible, have you ever seen any place where they leave you in peace, ever seen a place where they just let you lie down and say "so long?" they never forget about you, pal, don't worry, they're keeping an eye on you, prodding you in the ass, they won't leave you in peace, they've got to move you on, got to tell you to "go there" and there you go, "now go over there" and over there you go, "get your ass out of here," and you start packing your bags, me, when I was still working I used to spend the day packing my bags, work is always somewhere else, it's always somewhere else you gotta go to find it, no time to explain, no time for dreaming, no time to lie down somewhere in the grass and say "so long!", they move you on with a few kicks in the butt, work is over there, further on over there, further and further away 'til they push and prod you all the way to Nicaragua, which is easy enough, since the people from places like that of course get poked in the ass till they land here, whereas work, now, that's always some-where else, and you can never just say "so long, I'm home now" (which is how why whenever I leave a place, I always feel like I'm leaving a place which is more of a home than wherever it is I'm heading, and when they poke you and poke you in the ass again and again, and again you have to leave, wherever it is you're heading you'll be even more of a stranger, you're always less and less at home, they keep poking and prodding you further and further away until you don't even know where it is you're going, and one day you turn around, friend, you look behind you, and everything's a desert), but what if we just stopped once and for all and said: fuck off you bastards I am not budging another inch and you're going to hear me out, and what if we lie down somewhere in the grass once and for all and take the time to explain ourselves to each other, and you tell your story and the ones who've been kicked here all the way from Nicaragua or wherever, they'll tell you theirs , and we say to ourselves finally that we're all more or less strangers, but so long! 'cause now we're gonna listen to each other, then you'll really see things like I've seen them, that they don't give a good god-damn about us, and me, once I stopped and lis-tened, I told myself that as long as they don't give a damn about us, I'm not gonna work anymore, what good is it if Nicaragua comes all the way here, or if I go all the way over there, since everywhere elsewhere is all the same, and when I was still work-ing I talked about my plan for an international union of all the people who land here kicked-in-the-ass from god-knows-where to look for work, and they listened to me, and I listened to the Nicaraguans who told me about their home, like over there there's an old general who spends every day and every night at the edge of a forest, where they bring him his food so he doesn't have to leave, and this guy shoots at anything that moves, they bring him ammunition whenever he runs out, and they told me about this general and his troops who surround the forest back there and who takes target practice at anything that flies up above the tree-tops, at anything that appears at the edge of the forest, or at anything they spot which has a slightly different color than the trees or which doesn't move in quite the same way, and they listened to me and I listened to them, and, I said to myself: it's all the same anywhere else, and the more I let myself get poked in the ass, the more of a stranger I'll be, they end up here and I end up there—there where everything that moves is taking cover in the mountains, by the lakes, in the forests, while a general and his troops scour the mountains, patrol the lakes, surround the forests and take target practice at anything that flies up, anything that scampers, anything that moves, anything with a different color or movement than the rocks, the water, and the trees, I listened to all that and I stopped, I'm not gonna budge another inch, and I say: hope is here and if there's no work then I just won't work, if work drives me crazy and they start to poke me in the ass, then I just won't work anymore, I want to lie down somewhere, explain myself once and for all, I want grass and the shade under some trees, I want to shout and be able to shout, even if they have to start shooting, because that's what they end up doing: if you don't agree, if you open your trap, you've got to take cover somewhere deep inside a forest, and they'll mow you down with machine-guns the minute they spot you moving, so what the hell, who cares? at least I would've told you what I needed to tell you, I can't seem to manage that here, but maybe somewhere else, in a room, say, where we could spend the night, or anyway part of the night, since of course I'll leave before dawn, before you get fed up I'll leave just in time, before you want to leave yourself, 'cause if you got fed up and left me in the lurch, personally I'm not the sensitive type, to be bothered by any of it (and you can do whatever you like), but some of these muscle-bound guys, you take the most muscle-bound bone-crusher there is who doesn't bullshit or anything and who'll stomp the crap out of you without batting an eye at the sight of blood, not oversensitive or anywhere near it (the kind of bone-crusher you wouldn't mind being ignored by when he starts to get excited), well now with these guys, if you calmly pick up a needle, walk over without any fuss or bother and just prick them ever so slightly in the arm, and all of a sudden they see a tiny drop of blood (of their own blood right there in the middle of the calm, without getting them excited and for no reason) the biggest muscle-bound bone-crusher there is will turn white, collapse in a heap, and faint dead away over some trifle like that, whereas me now, I'm not the sensitive type, you'd split right away, and anyway that's not the only thing, but also that you'd take me for a nobody, and I couldn't really blame you today, today things aren't going so hot, I can't really feel all that pleased, not like the guys around here who always have such a pleased look about them, always ready to enjoy themselves, whereas for me, see, there's always something in the back of my head, something which always comes back to me without warning, stories about a forest somewhere where nothing dares to move because of the machine guns, or stories about some crazy old whore being buried somewhere completely unnoticed, whereas the guys around here they've got nothing in the back of their heads, they're always ready, ready to be pleased and ready for a good time, ready to get off all they can, anyplace anytime, don't give a thought about anything else except their little quickies, all those French assholes ready to get off on their own little quickies in their own little corner without anything in the back of their heads to get in the way, they flaunt it everywhere and come all over the place, come right in our faces, whereas me, now, I've got these stories in the back of my head, oh I can't say it never works, it's more like I'm the kind of guy who never completely gets off on account of these stories, sometimes I even feel pretty good, really good, like right now as long as you don't split and as long as I've got enough time, but back there in my head there's something sad in a way I wouldn't even know how to begin to explain, and with that story too you'd probably get fed up ('cause today probably I'm an absolute nobody, but one

of these days, you wait and see!), and you'd probably split before-
hand, but then I'm not the sensitive type (and you can do whatever you like), but god knows what I'd tell myself then, that
I'd rather be anything that isn't a tree, hidden away deep inside
a forest in Nicaragua, like a tiny bird who wants to fly up above
the tree-tops surrounded by rows of soldiers pointing their
machine-guns at it and watching for any kind of movement,
what I'm saying is I'm not gonna manage to say it here, we've
got to find some grass somewhere where we can lie down with
the whole sky over our heads in the shade of some trees, or
maybe where we can spend some time together, so in case you
think it's only a room I'm looking for, you're wrong, I'm not
sleepy, and nothing's easier to find than a room for the night,
the streets are full of room-hunters and room-suppliers for
the night, and if you think it's only to talk, you're wrong again,
I don't need that like those assholes out there, I'm not one of
them, personally instead of talking I'd rather follow a beautiful girl just to look at her, simply look at her, why do anything
else with a beautiful girl except look at her, and really I'm the
kind of guy who'd rather just walk around than look at a beautiful girl, that's enough for me for an occupation, all my life I
really just want to walk around, maybe jog a little from time to
time or stop on a bench somewhere, walk a little slower now
and then, now and then a little faster, without ever saying a
word, but with you it's not the same, and so the moment I saw
you, and now that I've said it I've got to explain it all without
you splitting and leaving me like an asshole, even if right now
I do look like mess and my hair and clothes won't dry out and
I wouldn't even want to look in that mirror behind my back,
whereas you, the rain didn't even get you wet, it just passed
right by you, time passes right by you, and that's why I was right
when I understood that you're nothing but a child and everything passes you right by, nothing moves and nothing looks like
a mess, whereas me now, I avoid mirrors and can't stop looking at you, you, the one who doesn't change, and if it weren't

for this money problem I'd buy us a beer instead of coffee, that way we'd really be set, we'd drink a few just like I've been wanting to since the beginning of the evening, I already had one, then another, maybe three or four more, I don't know, and all the money I wanted to spend we'd spend together right now, if it weren't for the fact that they stole it from me while ago, I had enough to drink all the beer you could want, all night long, enough to start feeling really nice, but they stole it down in the subway, that was a real dirty trick 'cause nothing's left for the whole night but the little bit of change I had in my front pocket, just enough for a couple of coffees, and yet I'm the one who ran up behind them, you'd almost think I was asking for it, and finally they stole it from me and beat me up to boot, down there in the subway corridor a couple of these punks with the kind of face you can't mistake, punks out on the prowl and looking for action, a pair of really flashy punks who make a point of dressing to the hilt, and I run up behind them and say to myself: we can go have ourselves a beer together, punks so flashy I've always wanted to run up behind them and say: give me your clothes, your shoes, your hair, your way of walk-ing, your face, just as they are, don't change a thing (and if they did give them to me I wouldn't even look back to see what I'd become), but they never noticed me, still I can't take my eyes off them and I get into the first train right behind them, say-ing to myself, I'll ask them out for a beer, we'll spend the evening together and all have a good time—but at that very second I feel one of them behind me slipping his hand into my back pocket and pulling out my wallet, at first I don't even move, I feel like keeping up appearances, then finally I say to myself: o.k. man, I don't want any trouble, I'll just talk to them, there's no reason why that shouldn't work, so I turn around and say: o.k., don't be an asshole, let me buy you a beer and later on we'll decide what we'll do together, and we'll all have a good time—the punk behind me looks at his buddy, they don't say a word and pretend they don't even see me—o.k. don't play dumb, give me back my money and let's go have a drink, go talk it over and then all together we'll go on to something else from there—they're still looking at each other as if they didn't understand, and then, little by little, just by exchanging a few glances, like this, they come to some kind of understanding, and they start saying, louder and louder so that everyone can hear, still without even looking at me: what's this guy want, anyway? is he lookin' for trouble, or what? who the fuck does he think he is? what's he buggin' us for?—and they push me towards the door: let's get this faggot off at the next stop and stomp the shit out of him so then I say to them: o.k., o.k., just gimme back my money and we'll call it quits, but there they are saying: you watch, this faggot's gonna get the shit kicked out of him—and nobody reacts, nobody believes in the money, everybody believes in the faggot, and I get dropped off at the next stop and when they've finished stomping the shit out of me like the lowest kind of faggot, and after they've run off with all my money (in spite of the fact that I'm screaming, nobody believes it), then I don't move right away: I say above all, man, don't get excited, sit down on the bench and don't move, stay right here—I look around and I listen, that's all, everything's gonna be fine: there's some music in the distance behind me, a busker playing for handouts (it's okay, man, above all, just don't move), on the opposite platform there's an old crone sitting there all dressed up in yellow smiling and gesturing (I'm watching and listening, everything's still all right) and on the rail upstairs there's this lady who suddenly stops dead in her tracks to catch her breath, right next to me some Arab sits down and starts singing all this Arab stuff softly to himself (I'm saying to myself: above all, man, there's still no reason to get excited), and right in front of me I see, I swear I'm absolutely positive that I see a girl in a white nightgown with her hair all down her back, right in front of me, she walks by with her fists clenched in her white nightgown, and right in front of me all of a sudden her face begins to break up and she starts to cry, she walks on down to the end of the platform with her hair all undone and her fists balled up like this, in her nightgown, and then, all of a sudden, this time I've had it, that's it, I can't take it anymore, I've had it with everyone around here, with everyone and his little story in his little corner, had it with all of their faces, had it with all of them, and suddenly all I want to do is beat up something or somebody, that lady up there leaning on the rail I'd really like to belt her one, this Arab singing his shit there all alone to himself, him, too, I really want to clobber him, I want to beat up that pauper back down at the end of the corridor, and the old crone on the other side, I've had it with their faces and with the whole circus, with that girl in her nightgown at the end of the platform who's still wailing, and now I am going to slug something, man I want to belt somebody, anybody, the old crones, the Arabs, the paupers, the tile walls, the rows of cars, the conductors, the cops, beat up the coin machines, the posters, the lights, the god-damned stink and the god-damned noise, and I'm thinking about all those glasses of beer I drank and all of the ones I would've drunk until my stomach couldn't take anymore, man, I kept sitting there with this urge to beat up something or somebody until it all stops moving, and then, all of a sudden, everything does stop moving: the trains stop going by, the Arab stops singing, the lady up on the rail stops breathing, and the girl in the nightgown stops sniffling, everything stops all at once except for the music from the rear and the old crone whose mouth is now wide open starts to sing in a terrifying voice, and when the pauper behind me plays something, she sings it in response, they answer each other back and forth and then come together just like they had it all rehearsed (terrifying music, some kind of opera or stuff like that), but so loud and so together that everything truly has come to a stop and the voice of the old crone fills the entire place, and me, I say: okay, that's it—I get up and scoot through the corridor, bound up the stairs, fly out into the air and start running, still dreaming about beer and running, about beer, about beer, and

I say to myself: what a circus with all this opera and these women, the cold choking dirt, the girl in the nightgown, the whores and the cemeteries, and I'm running completely out of my head now, looking for something like grass in the middle of this garbage, the doves fly up above the forest and the soldiers shoot them down, paupers play for handouts, flashy punks hunt for sand-niggers, I run and run and run, I dream of those secret songs among the Arabs, brothers, and finally I find you and take you by the arm, I want a room so much and I'm all wet, mama, mama, mama, don't say a word, don't move, I look at you and I love you, brother, sister, me, I'm looking for some-one like an angel in the middle of this circus and there you are, I love you and so on, some beer and some more beer, I still don't know how I could ever say it, what a mess, what a circus, brother, and then always still the rain, the rain, the rain...

∾

Michel Azama

The Sifter

Translated from the French by
Judith G. Miller

UBU REPERTORY THEATER PUBLICATIONS
NEW YORK

Michel Azama, born in 1947, holds a Master's degree in modern literature from The University of Montpellier-Paul Valéry. He trained at the Jacques Lecoq School and with the Simon Program in Paris and subsequently acted for several years in various French regional companies. He worked for many years at the National Dramatic Center of Dijon, of which he became dramaturg in 1990. In 1993, he left the Dijon Center to become Editor-in-Chief of the drama revue *Les Cahiers de Prospero,* which is published by the National Center for Dramatic Writing at the Chartreuse in Villeneuve-lez-Avignon. As teacher and coach, he has frequently worked with actors on performance techniques. He has also directed many writing workshops for beginning playwrights. Michel Azama has published numerous dramatic texts, including: *Bled, Vie et Mort de Pier Paolo Pasolini, Le Sas, Croisades, Iphigénie ou le péché des dieux, Aztèques, Les deux terres d'Akhenaton, Zoo de nuit* (with Editions Théâtrales); and *Amours fous* (in *Brèves d'auteurs,* with Editions Actes Sud Papiers). All his plays were premiered in France. They have been translated into several languages and produced in many different countries, notably Germany, Switzerland, England, Brazil, Argentina, Spain and Holland. In 1986 he won the Prix des Trois Provinces—a drama prize awarded for a text from France, Belgium, or Quebec—for *The Sifter (Le Sas).* In 1994 his play, *Zoo de nuit,* received the prestigious Prix Beaumarchais.

Judith G. Miller is professor of French and Francophone theater at The University of Wisconsin-Madison. She has published widely on French-language theater, bringing out recently with Christiane Makward: *Plays by French and Francophone Women: A Critical Anthology* (The University of Michigan Press, 1994), which includes texts by Corinna Bille, Denise Boucher, Ina Césaire, Chantal Chawaf, Andrée Chedid, Hélène Cixous, Michèle Foucher, and Antonine Maillet, in addition to an annotated bibliography of theater texts by women. For Ubu Repertory Theater Publications, she has translated plays by Ina Césaire and Werewere Liking published in *Plays by Women: An International Anthology, Book Two* and *New French-Language Plays*. She is currently preparing, for the Feminist Press, a reader based on Werewere Liking's work. Judith Miller also directs and produces French and Francophone plays with students at Wisconsin.

AUTHOR'S NOTE

How did I come to write *The Sifter?*

My play, *The Life and Death of Pasolini,* was being performed in Paris at the Essaïon Theater when an advisor from the Ministry of Culture, who had attended one of the performances, came looking for me, saying, "Apparently you're not afraid of violent worlds. Would you be interested in running a theater workshop in prison?"

That's how I found myself in the central women's prison in Rennes, one of France's worst prisons, working with a dozen prisoners, eight hours a day for fifteen days.

The prisoners had chosen to come to my workshop. And I had asked to work without any surveillance from the guards, in order for the women to feel free to speak to me about whatever they wanted.

Since we were working in a room situated right in the middle of an old Napoleonic prison shaped like a hexagon, which afforded no opportunities for escape, the authorities left me alone with the prisoners. This prison is reserved for women who have been sentenced to four years or more. Two of the women in my group had been given life sentences for crimes of passion.

We prepared a short piece that they finally performed for three hundred other prisoners, with all the prison guards standing against the walls, their black rubber billy clubs in their hands in case the performance set off some kind of vague revolt.

But what was crucial to me wasn't the performance. What was crucial happened during the rehearsals, where we took our many breaks. It was during the breaks that little by little they opened up to me: little anecdotes about prison life, its humiliations, its traumas, the thousand and one vexations and even, you might say, the thousand and one ways of not respecting the most elementary of human dignities.

Every evening I took notes.

When I left, overwhelmed, having understood from the inside just how false all discourses on prison end up being, I was very worked up. What should I do with my notes? How could I avoid the traps looming before me? How could I speak about a women's prison as a poet, or a theater person, and not like a reporter? How could I, a man, and free, find the right words to communicate everything about that institution which is disgusting, barbarous, a denial of civilization?

That's when I remembered what one of the guards told me: prisoners kill themselves especially at the end of their sentence because the fear of what's waiting for them on the outside becomes too great. That's how I found the dramatic situation which made it possible to write: a woman's last night in prison, after sixteen years of incarceration. One night in the celebrated short-timers' cell, that "sifter" between the inside and the outside, the kind of night in which one inevitably has nightmares, confused images, memories of a traumatic past, of the trial, of the thousand happy and sad anecdotes of prison life, and especially, the inevitable phantasmatic and frightening projection of the future waiting on the other side, lurking like a monster whose terrifying snout is all that's visible: unemployment, solitude, perhaps illness because of incompetently treated pain, rejection by one's family, difficulties in loving and being loved, etc., etc.

I didn't want to invent any facts: what exists is already terrible enough. My work as a writer consisted in placing a woman in a dramatic situation—the last night before release—and giving her a more imaginative, more fiery language than in reality. It's in singing one's pain that one exorcises it. And that's what I wanted to create: an oratorio from which pain escapes, a cry traveling towards us, free human beings, the living, a cry uttered by a dead woman, a cry which awakens, which asks questions, which frightens, because the theater must not simply please its audience; we must frighten it if we want theater to be something more than entertainment.

When Chantal Deruaz, the magnificent actress who created the play, was ready to perform the text in public for the first time, she insisted on doing so in prison, because she needed some kind of approval from the prisoners, a sort of guarantee to feel she had the right to say the words. She performed in the municipal prison for men in Béthune, for three hundred hardened criminals who were all in tears at the end of the show. Theater had again achieved its miracle: it was stronger than real life, because these men, who had never before cried, at least in public, over their status as outcasts, cried when faced with the representation of their misfortune. Catharsis took place.

Since then, the text has been performed a lot, by many actresses, and seen by quite a number of former prisoners. Each time the actresses, as well as those who know what prison is, tell me the same thing: the pain of which the text speaks is also our pain, the pain of free human beings, the pain of lonely human beings, without love, unable to cope with the future, disarmed when faced with the past, and yet alive, yes, inevitably alive.

MICHEL AZAMA

A Cell.
Naked white walls stage right and left. A toilet. A stool. A plank
bed leaning against one wall. A door downstage with a cop-
per peephole which is sprung open noisily from time to time. A
very high transom with opaque glass.
This space can also be created without recourse to realism.
The audio environment alone will bring the prison to life: steps
in the corridor. Noises of locks opening and closing. Screams.
Echoing sounds of breaking glass. Heating pipes rapping and
knocking...
The play begins in the middle of the night and ends at dawn.

THE SHORT-TIMER:
What's that telegram?
I asked the social worker.
The night before getting out you're a mess.
A Minister who's sacked, a President who croaks you never know.
Over nothing they cancel your pardon, your file's been shelved
they say.
You're not being released.

Something like that, anyway...

I didn't think of you for a second, Mama.

"They've cancelled my parole," I said.

She was having trouble. I finally got it.
No she said with her head.
So I swallowed hard. I stayed very calm:
I screamed, I think, "No."
"*You* read it," I said.
"I'm sorry, I'm so sorry," she repeated.
Like a record.

I said again, yelling (no, in a soft voice)
"Read it."
And I added, habit I guess, "Please."
"It's your mother," she finally said.
"Her heart. She didn't have time to suffer."

I must have screamed one more time. I don't know. After that
I think I fainted.

Be brave.
Sixteen years I've been waiting. Not the time to go to pieces
over a few hours.

You always knew that life had more shit in store for you.

Funny spot, here, between two worlds.
The short-timers' cell. Outside they never say short-timer.

That door, there, which leads to the entrance courtyard.
The entrance courtyard closed in by swinging gates which I
haven't passed through for sixteen years. Swinging gates which
lead to the street. The street...

Don't be afraid, baby, hold yourself up by the bootstraps. Getting
out is nothing, get that through your skull. It's nothing, the rest
is over, behind you, you're done with it, sixteen times done with
it.
It doesn't matter, Mama, you shouldn't have done it, such a
lousy trick the day they let me out.
So it's true then, never finished with the muck, it sticks to you
for life.
Nicole always said so: she used to call it, "muckup."
"Girl," she'd say, "take it from one who's been out lots of
times, it's when you step out of this joint that all hell falls on
your head, you'll see."

"Get your things ready, you're being transferred."
"But when, Ma'am? Nobody said anything to me yesterday."
"You want to make something of it? They're waiting for you over there. Hurry up. You have an hour."

I was all right there. In the holding pen. My cell mate is crying in silence. I gather my things without looking at her. I would've been happy to stay a while longer.

Even though it stinks, even though any thing can set your nerves on edge. There's talking, there's laughing, there's crying, there's life.
Whores, thieves, murderesses, bag ladies, hold-up artists, butchers, kid killers, it's a cross between bordello and loony bin but it's alive. The tin plates, the chalky soap (what do they make that soap from, anyway?), the strings tied from bed to bed loaded with underwear, the nervous fits, the screeching boom boxes, the ass-hole stories, the cheap perfume, the lice and the filth of the street tramps and all night long, the anguish strolling from bed to bed and coming back at you ten times the speed like a boomerang.
Yeah, I was all right there. Warm... My pain melting in with everybody else's.

Where I'm going, nobody knows. Just a bunch of "they say's" and made-up stories, nobody knows.
Even the city folk out there, they don't know. It's another world. A cross between the morgue and the convent.

Gérard, Gilbert, I'll be far away, I won't see you grow up.

Frisked again. Bound. The police van.
Stay cool, good God, think about something else. Look. Streets, squares, people. After all those months of concrete, you might even fall in love with a tree.

Ten o'clock. Departure time. Watch your step!
At the station, people turn their heads away. A woman in hand-cuffs between two cops makes them uncomfortable. A young dark type smiles at me. I chew my lip.
Let's go. Open your eyes. Tighten your butt. Straighten up. Look. I look as though devouring. The thickets, the Rhone, the absolutely yellow mustard field, the flowering apple tree. Register it. Stuff the landscapes in your brain. Tomorrow you'll put them where the walls are. You'll look at this every day for twenty years. Those rivers full of pebbles. That junk yard for cars. I wish I were a pile of metal rusting away some place, forgotten.
Look! A vineyard. A whole childhood of vineyards.
I look. I look. I look. It's unbelievable all these simple things. The color of the sky can never be named. It changes every minute.

There, I'll only see the color of the uniforms and white walls like a clinic's. A vegetable garden embraced by walls. That word, 'wall'...
A red roadside tavern in yellow fields.
You and I often ate in roadside taverns, maybe even in that one...
It must be National Highway number 9. Night's here.
The car lights on the trees that dot the landscape.
What will I see of the sky there, a tiny little square in the exercise yard.
My face in the window. I'm thirty-three years old. An entombment. Go ahead cry.
It doesn't matter any more.
The cop says softly: "Want a cigarette? It's usually not allowed but..."
And that makes me cry even more.
He has a mustache. I say, "Do you have children?"
Gérard, Gilbert, when will I see you again?

How old will you be?

He talks about his oldest who's doing bad in school. He smiles.

He says: "Are you feeling better?"

Yeah, I'm O.K. I'm really fine. I'm totally dead.

This is it, we're there. Three-minute stop. Twenty-year stop. I stood up, I remember, to take a better look.

The double door with its giant nails shining in the headlights. Both sides swing wide open.

The police van enters the courtyard. I turn around. The door closes slowly. All by itself. It must be electric. I still see the street by the light of the street lamp. A man goes by with a baguette under his arm. I won't see a man again.

"Take your clothes off."

I take off my sweater, skirt, panty hose, panties, and bra.

"What's that medal there?"

"Just a medal, Ma'am."

"You have permission for it? No? Give it here."

"No, Ma'am."

"Don't start! You're not here for your good looks. Give it to me."

"No, Ma'am."

"We've made plenty of others cooperate, you know."

She pulls on it. The chain breaks. It stings. I have a red mark on my neck. I put my stuff back on. I cover myself. I'm ashamed. You'll get used to it, sweetheart, you'll get used to it. Showing your ass is no big deal.

In the end it's your heart that's naked and that's a lot worse.

Not a single cig to drag on. Buried alive. Hello! Hello up there! Calling planet Earth.

"Shut your trap." You're in the welcome unit.

"You're not allowed to gab through the windows. Or else, you'll be in big trouble."

"But..."

"Shut your trap." You're being put in solitude for three weeks' observation.

They call that a welcome. Some kind of welcome. The bed clamped to the floor. The stool clamped to the floor. The transom too high up. The windows nailed shut. The slot where the screws slide your chow in. An hour walk in a pie-sized sliver. If you see a bird, it's your lucky day. Observation. A rat in a cage. Death digs its mole's way through my body. Hey. My period is really late. The nightmare. Always the same. A man. He holds my hand. He looks like you. I have a bouquet of flowers. I'm happy. He leads me through the streets of an unknown city. He leaves me all of a sudden and disappears around a corner. I look for him, scared out of my wits. Nobody. I run. My legs won't carry me any more. Night falls all of a sudden, just like in the movies. The city's completely deserted and silent.
Two men emerge from a huge door, running. They grab me, push me inside. I scream. I recognize the prison. I want to run. My legs are made of lead. They chuckle. They undress me.
"Raise your leg! Some of 'em hide things in there."
On his knees one of them looks up my vagina, the other spreads my buttocks with his hands. I wake up in a sweat. My heart beats fast for hours. That girl who was crossing the courtyard with her things on a trolley. A short-timer. Suitcases, badly tied boxes. She'd just come back from properties. We hollered to her gaily: "Good luck, good luck, don't look back when you pass those doors." The result: No walks for fifteen days.

"Pull your pants down!"
We do it.
"Sleep!"
And we sleep.
"If you're here it's because you asked for it."
And we say, "Yes, Ma'am..."
If we're good, they'll like us. We'll be rewarded.

Or they can put us in the hell hole. Forbid dessert and movies. Put us in a padded cell, on a diet of stale bread and water. It's for our own good. Our rehabilitation. To teach us how to live like normal persons. And to be normal, for our own good, since we're all little girls, we have to be scolded, scolded, scolded...

"You're pretty cool, Ma'am. It's easy to see you're young. Can I call you by your first name?"

"No way. They might try to can me," the small screw said. "If a supervisor noticed. Just think... They might even suspect..."

"What?"

"Well...plotting, homosexuality, how do I know... No, you have to call me 'Ma'am'..."

They stuck me in group 3. The fat girls' group. If you aren't already, you get to be one.

No rights to gym. Nothing to keep you busy. After shop, alone in your cell from 2 p.m. 'till the next morning. Stuffing yourself with bread. Waiting. In the cell.

"By the way," the Warden says, "we don't say 'cell' here, we say 'room'."

Your behavior wasn't too good in solitude: broken windows, nervous fits, insulting the guards, hysteria. Bull-headed. Shut up! You don't think we'll let you take courses, do you? Courses are for people who're civilized. We're putting you in house-keeping. Assigned to clean-up. It's great exercise for somebody like you who's got too much energy.

Shut up! Of course you make less than in the shop. And don't tell me you're weak or sick. You're never too sick to act like a fool. Shut up! We're deducting your pension and social security, the rest will be divided in two. One half for tampax, toilet products, stamps, butter, sugar, chocolate, and so on as well as the clothes you choose from the mail order house.[1] The other half goes for administrative costs. You pay room and board here like everywhere else. Three-fifths for food, one-fifth for legal costs, and one-fifth for the nest egg you claim upon release. So that's it. And you should understand refusing to talk doesn't work in your favor. It's just another behavioral problem we'll have to cite in your file. Putting on airs won't help either.

Shut up! If you continue being so negative, my friend, and you stay in group 3, you won't be able to buy much with your nest egg when you get out: nothing plus nothing adds up to nothing. Even after twenty years. Now you know. No. You'll speak when you're told to. Of course they're going to take your children away. You've lost your maternal rights. They'll be under the jurisdiction of social welfare.[2] With foster families. Your mother's too old to take care of them, even though she asked to.

So?

You still don't want to say anything?

I only caught on later, naturally. The carrot trick. You do what you're supposed to, and surprise! You don't have to work on national holidays. Submissive, surprise! You're promoted to group 2. Edgy, watch out! You're demoted. Returned to the mop house. Their little pecking order. Above there's group 1. Above that a little confidence in you. Above that full confidence. You become responsible for the chapel, the infirmary, the library.

Still above that, semi-freedom. Work outside, sleep inside.

And be careful not to linger between work and sleep. Or else...

And above all that, parole: you're released before your sentence is up.

So watch out, be careful what you do. It's pretty easy to shelve a case. A file can drag between here and the courts...

In the beginning you're always in group 3. Fat girls, mops, potato peels, garbage, maybe group 2, never higher.

You have to be able to hope for something. A goal. Getting out is too far away. If you had their full confidence right away, the social worker says, you'd end up thinking about suicide.

You're hiding yourself in words, and then singing them under

your breath, admit it. You're picking your scabs to forget how scared you are. In less than a few hours, you'll be out.
At daybreak, you'll be back on the scene. It's the last hurdle, you've got to be able to handle it.

I spit out the goddam tranquilizer. With time you really get good at it. You stick it between your cheek and your teeth, the screw can make you drink all she wants. As soon as she leaves, you spit it out. I don't want to sleep, to lose an instant of tonight. Spend it eyes open, be on my feet to say so long to these bars when I hear the morning bells for the last time.
Your walls have melted tonight. They don't exist any more. They've completely disappeared. This time it's true, the dream will last beyond the night. And in the morning, the door really will open onto the street. There'll be cars, men going to work in their blue work clothes, in ties; a woman will be pushing a baby carriage, I'll try to see the baby over her shoulder.
Life.
I'll run errands, I'll go to a bistro, I'll be served like a normal person. Will I know how to pay?
Lost the habit of bills, change, doors to open—pull...push.
Nicole told me the first time you get out, you act completely stupid in front of doors, as if you were waiting for a screw to come and open them.
"Good day, Sir, I'm an accountant. I saw your ad."
"Do you have references, Madam? Where was your last job?"
How to erase it. Make it go away...
"What's your address, we'll contact you."
"St. Ursula's Foyer..."
"Isn't that the foyer for..."
"That's right, ex-prisoners."

How to erase the blood?
It wasn't them who stuck me in here, I did it to myself. I'm paying for my mistake; when I get out, I'll walk tall, I'll look

people straight in the eye. I'll have paid. I won't owe anything to anybody.

You think like that for years. But when you get ready to leave, it's not so easy, scared shitless. Gérard, I haven't seen you since you went into the army. And Gilbert since boarding school. In four years you change a lot at your age. Gérard's first visiting day... I'd been here three years. To see him, I had to cut through all the red tape at social services.

I got all dolled-up, had my hair done, a good dress.

"So what's this, are you getting married or something?" Nicole joked.

"Better than that, babe. My son's going to be at visiting hours. My oldest.

I haven't seen him for three years."

"How old he is now?"

"Seven. He was four when I screwed up."

"He won't recognize you."

"Don't say that. I can't believe how scared I am."

I came back in tears, eye makeup running, hair all over the place.

"What happened to you? He didn't come?"

"Oh yes he did. Worse than that. He screamed, hit me, bit, kicked the doors. He wanted me to leave with him. They couldn't control him. He knocked chairs over, threw himself at the walls. They had to shorten the visit. He would've killed himself banging his head against the tables. I saw him for fifteen minutes. I don't know when I'll see my kid again."

I write. I write. I write.

I scribble to myself. I have to make the time go by.

In the evening I sleep with my letters and the next day I tear them up. Your last note, Nicole. Yesterday's. Our last walk together. It took me a long time to tell you exactly when I was getting out.

It wasn't easy. We bawled like two crazy ladies. You crossed your

fingers to ward off bad luck.
"Which shower stall are you in?"
"Number 4, Ma'am."
"Where's Nicole then?"
"She's in 4, Ma'am."
"I'm reporting this."
"We're not doing anything, Ma'am, we're washing up."
"You'll wash up better in solitary."
The sweet voice of Boss Lady.
They think the least little tenderness is fooling around.
"Called a guard a horny bitch, an ugly slut, and a baboon."
"Gave a bar of chocolate to another prisoner who accepted."
"Covered the window of her cell with her bedspread."
"Stopped up the peephole with bread dough."
"Wore a sweater during the exercise period."
"Broke her bowl."
"Exchanged notes with another prisoner. Swallowed the note rather than show it to the guard."
"You wouldn't be walking with Nicole, would you? It's O.K., you know, as long as it doesn't go too far."

"Yes, Ma'am. I'm walking with Nicole. Every day. An hour in the exercise yard."
"Don't trust any of your pals. Jeanine is a liar, Marie-Laure is only out for herself, Paulette's a hypocrite. You'll see, when they get out they'll forget all about you. Prisoners are immature, selfish, wishy-washy, fickle."
"Oh, Ma'am, you're a brunette now, you look better that way."
"Oh, Ma'am, you gained some weight on your vacation."
They watch us, sitting there all morning for seven hours without budging, without the right to read or do anything else; what a job. They watch us but we see them.

I say yelling (no, in a very soft voice)
Read it. And I add, habit I guess, please.

She said, "Wouldn't you know—today. What bad luck."
Yes. I already know that. I tore the telegram from her hands and I read.
It said, "Mother died yesterday. Funeral tomorrow."
There was no signature. For no reason, maybe to feel better, I screamed. No, I don't remember, I was very calm. It was too much for her, I said. Her heart, the excitement of my release. After, yes, it was after that I screamed. I think.
"Don't believe that, it was her age," the social worker said. "God didn't mean for her to see you again."
"God. You know what you can do with God?"
"Don't say such a thing," she said. Had to say something.
"They'll be waiting for you for the funeral."
For the funeral?
Don't count on me. Call. Do what you want, but I'm not getting out of here to go to my mother's funeral. You hear me? God.
How about a break? By now if you existed...
Just a little break. A sign. Am I so old, ugly, sterile.
At the end of the trail. Never able to feel love again.
God.
Yeah. You asked for it. Yeah. It's my fault. I accept all the blame. I make no excuses. The dirtiest, sickest, most awful. Every act. I don't deny it, no. I did it. I did it. It's me, only me. Yes, yes, yes. Me. The blood shed, the dried blood on that cloth. The proof of what I did exhibited. The locks, the murmurs of the crowd, the cage, they call it. That square box in the wings of the courtroom. I wait.
You're eight men and one woman. I would've preferred more women. Maybe they would've understood me better. You'll never get it, you can never sort out what the witnesses say, the bitterness, the jealousy, the hate.
"I don't feel well."
"You're O.K., don't worry about it. You're just nervous," my lawyer says.

The experts, the personality specialists. Those who say "my dear," those who say "Madam," all come to see the animal.
In the court's hallways my high heels sound like the rhythms of busy mice.
The first night they left some hot tea in my cell.
I couldn't swallow anything. Telegrams as though I were a movie star.
Sleep, impossible... Blood, that blood-stained cloth right out there, proof of what I did for all the world to see. The jury stares at it all the time. The maximum. That's what's waiting for you, my dear. Those hands being raised, swearing to tell the truth. All of it. Nothing but. It'll last three days. You have to hang in there, says the head matron.
"And don't be so stiff," says the lawyer. "They don't like that. Don't keep pulling your shoulders back, it gives you airs."
Reporters. A full house. What a show. I don't dare catch the eye of the only woman juror.
Who is she?
Who are you, Ma'am? Have any children?
My life since birth. On display. A file thicker than the Paris phone book.

"Her grandfather blew his head off with a rifle."
"What are they getting at?"
"Everything matters," says the chief guard. "Your grandfather's story doesn't make you look so good."
"But it has nothing to do with anything."
"Family history makes a difference."
"But..."
"It's all the blood."
"Sir, do you think they're going..."
"Take it easy."
"But the prosecuting attorney looks so mean."
"That's his job."
The women all wore their best spring outfits for the witness stand.

Beauty shop, jewelry. Maybe they hoped they'd get on TV.
So many witnesses to listen to every day. I'm exhausted.
My guard's counting witnesses. Four more left. Then two.
Stay alert. Now it's the defense witnesses' turn. But it's too late,
nobody's listening. It's already dark.
A flood of lost words. Convict me right away. Let's get it over
with. I don't want to come back tomorrow. My private life
depicted as a horror story.
"Even as a little girl, she liked to tear off her dolls' heads."
Now the defense, my life portrayed as angelic. I don't expect
anything. You've left. You're deliberating. Back there, in the
corner of a room, my life's between your hands.
"Ladies and gentlemen, the jury is returning!"
Everyone stands up, they motion to me.
I stand, it seems like a mass. I hurt everywhere. We sit down.
It's done. It's decided.
Yes, guilty. Yes, premeditation. I knew it.

The maximum.
Don't cry, don't buckle under. They're going to strafe you with
their flash bulbs when the judge reads out the sentence.
"In light of these proceedings, I see no evidence of attenuat-
ing circumstances and declare the accused guilty as charged.
The accused is sentenced to twenty years in prison."
"Twenty years! It's not possible, is it Sir? You said ten at the
most."
"You're lucky you didn't get life, don't complain."
Twenty years. Maybe I shouldn't have worn beige.

It suits you just fine, right Mister government men, those 40,000
cons in France's prisons? They slave for next to nothing and
never strike, they make prison guard uniforms, throw pillows,
stuffed animals, expensive ties. The scum slaving for the cream.
Seen from the other side, your justice is a real beaut. In your
bureaucratic jargon, you call it 'rehabilitation.' Sure. It's real

useful to know how to make stuffed animals when you get out. It's real easy to accumulate cushy savings at three francs a tie. You just have to stop smoking—you save on nicotine. And be illiterate—you save on magazines and stamps,—stop having your period—save on tampax,—control your cravings—save on butter, salt, and sugar. Alice...now Alice is one of the ones who's not going to be rich when she's released. She's turned her cell into a genuine love nest. Padded cover for her sanitary pail, flowered drapes, with sheers and matching bedspread, hung from upholstered drapery rods, white lace to hide the cathedral panes of the phony window, and there on the bed the model herself, a perfectly idealized very feminine at-home wife: the Queen of the harem[3] in a black negligee, posing like a star from an old movie magazine.[4] Trying to forget she's put on fifteen kilos.

A moan. It's a death rattle. Next door. I'm sure of it.
A death rattle. Marie-Laure. Marie-Laure? Marie-Laure?
My God, come quickly. She's going to cancel.

She pounds on the door and screams.

Where's the screw? What's she doing—sleeping?

We can hear the yells of the other women on the cellblock.

Ma'am, Ma'am, Ma'am.

Noise of footsteps in the corridor.

Marie-Laure, don't fuck up Marie-Laure.
Marie-Laure?
Oh! Ma'am. I thought you'd never get here. Look next door. It's Marie-Laure. Something's not right. No, don't go away. Look through the peep hole... Tell me, Ma'am, what is it? A scarf? Is

she strangling herself?

Marie-Laure, don't fuck up. There's nothing to it you'll see, don't be afraid, getting out is easy, you've been through the worst. Marie-Laure?

What are you waiting for to go in there? By the time a supervisor gets here, she'll be dead. Ma'am please. Go ahead. Screw the rules. Listen. The moaning's getting louder. Oh. Hurry up. What the hell are the supervisors doing? Did you phone them? Go on in anyway. They can't blame you for saving her life. Go on. Go in there.

> *Noise of running in the corridor. Then keys. A lot of voices speaking at once. Then an immense silence.*

You untied the scarf? Is she breathing? Tell me! Is she breathing? What's going on? Is the nurse there? What the fuck's she doing? I bet the Doc couldn't even be bothered to come? Dear God. Let her be O.K.

Sure they take care of us. Real good. Claire with her sore throat— I need an x-ray, Doctor.
And the Doc shrugs his shoulders.
"Get real. You just want a little vacation in the prison hospital. It's in your head. That's all. You've got prison-house disease."
When you get out, you rush for an x-ray. But it's too late. Cancer.

I'm cold.
Who'll be waiting for me in the morning when I get out?
Nobody.
Just one more night. Day'll be breaking soon, how do I get back in touch. Bond with my two sons. I've seen them about ten times in sixteen years. About thirty minutes each time, that makes...what...five hours? Five hours in sixteen years, it doesn't count for much in terms of tenderness. With the screw right

there. Always.

Gilbert, you screamed, you didn't know me.

Felt like breaking everything. Holding you next to me naked. Smelling you, licking you.

Dead for hours.

Don't keep saying "my babies" when you talk about them, the social worker said. Get used to the idea: they're men.

The oldest's doing his military service, the youngest has girl-friends. After all he's seventeen. They didn't wait for you to live. You won't be the center of their lives. Better get used to it. And so on.

"You're going to hate me, I know you will. Yes, you will. It's as if... I don't know how... I mean... I... It wasn't really me... As if somebody else was acting in my place. He'd left me, you see... No money, no job, no reason to live...

I opened my son's vein. The big one there on the neck where you feel the heart beating. With the tip of a kitchen knife. Just a nick. So it would run out slowly, so he wouldn't know he was dying.

I think it'll drive me nuts.

I've got a picture of him. Want to see it? He's beautiful don't you think? He was two years old."

Poor Annie, I liked you. I really did. One night in your cell, between shifts, you hung yourself. When the guard found you at 4 a.m., it was too late. We understood right away seeing how crazy everything got. The supervisors, the Warden, the screws, the Doc and the chaplain in the middle of the night. We knew. They let us see you one more time. The next day, the cof-fin making its way across the courtyard. It choked us up. Sylvie said, "That's how I'll leave this place." Sylvie's a lifer.

We had to calm her down. Make her drink something.

Jeanine said, "You won't be frisked this time, honey. You're get-ting out and you won't even know what it looks like out there."

Someone said, "They put us in the paupers' grave, that's the law."

And somebody else, "They could've tolled the death knell this morning. We're not animals, are we?"

Hurry up! Ladies we're going now. Hurry up take your seats. Hurry to mass.
Hurry even more if you want to earn something. Hurry to the mess hall to eat.
We're here for years but we never have any time.
One day nothing happens then the next day nothing happens.
Each night you say to yourself—that's another one down.
And every day's done as soon as it starts when I cross it off my calendar.
I know all about the lack of surprises, the boredom of watching the hours go by, I wait terrified for the moment between the last blackbird and the first star, when night enters the cell.
Hurry up, hurry up, recite poetry to yourself, hold conversations all alone. I get a running start and, pow, I'm way back there, far away swimming with you, we're rolling around in the sand. I don't know yet that one day I'll kill you.
Two shots...

Hurry up. Think of something else. It's my how-many Christmases inside? Julien, please turn the lamps on in all the drawing rooms, light all the chandeliers, add some candles when the first guests arrive, don't wait to uncork the champagne, it's Christmas tonight and I'm entertaining.
It's time for suicide attempts and broken windows. In the courtyard every falling window smashes with an unbelievable echo, it makes you want to do the same. Women scream. Other windows are busted. The screws run through the corridors and threaten us outside our doors, the pressure's enormous, forty women screaming in chorus, the whole cellblock. Everything's shaking, we're banging, shouting, out of our minds. The crazy ward. You never even noticed you'd bitten yourself.

A round table. Two children doing their homework. From time to time a woman joins them and bends over under the surrounding halo of light.

Ten years of my life to be that woman, just one evening.

A little girl plays with my children at the seashore, and that little girl is me.

I sit down next to them. My sons. My babies, my kids are always little. I walk with them on the beach, I caress the cheek of the oldest, I hold the little one's hand, I run my fingers through their hair, I laugh, I cry with them, we scream we want to die, we don't give a fuck about your tribunal, Madam Warden, your Hitler court where you can't even defend yourself, your concentration camp in skirts.

"You claim the guard is lying? That she's prejudiced when it comes to you? And you refuse to admit you did anything wrong?"

We don't give a shit about your punishments, your prolonging the time between pay dates, your demotions, your withholding of tobacco and your famous hell hole, the night belongs to us, Madam Warden. We call your hell hole Chamonix, it's freezing in there in winter, and in summer we call it St. Tropez, it makes us dream; night can't be put in prison, Madam Warden. Your hell hole is swell, that closet which scares little girls afraid of the dark—we drift through it easily, doped up on tranquilizers.

I'm holding a child, it's my son, he's so tiny, I bathe him, he's so beautiful naked like that, he laughs, he likes the way I touch him, he's still all mine, he holds me in his arms, I'm bareskinned against him, My God, isn't he just like a man?

I'm buying a bouquet of roses, Mama you're not dead and they're for you.

You know the worst, Madam Warden? I'm afraid my period will come back. I'm afraid to feel something again. I've lost the habit, I like it better this way. They say it comes back when you get out. In the beginning my period reassured me, made me feel better. Hey. My body hasn't forgotten the moon even if it never sees it. I'm still connected to the sky, still an animal, I have my tides. I put blood everywhere. I marked up my cell with ten red fingers, I got the hell hole because of all that blood, you even seemed disgusted by it, Madam Warden. I made a white flag with bloody red stripes. Because of that blood, I had an open window, doors, passageways, tunnels under the night, I got to play Good Buddy with Madam Solitude and Hide and Seek with Mister Future. One month nothing. An accident, I think. Two months nothing. The third month I told Nicole. It took me three whole months. She laughed. It's everybody's story, girl. After a few months, there's no more anything. Even the Docs don't get it. Of course they don't really try. They could give a fuck about our periods. For all the purpose they'd serve. Anyhow, I guess that's why, because we don't see any men. On the other hand, you have to admit you save on sanitary pads. That's when I felt dead.

And now to top it off, afraid it'll come back, that it'll start to flow again. I'm forty-nine years old, not quite fifty. Maybe I'm ugly now? Men—that was a long time ago.

Afraid of time's ravages. Breasts are O.K. I think. Ass can get by. Not too much cellulite. When I was in group 3 I gained fifteen kilos. All at once. It took me eight years to lose them. I don't know, but I guess you ought to be able to tell somehow, maybe the eyes.

People are going to say, that one over there she just got out. When you've got the walls inside you and your skin just barely covering them, it has to show. You get so hard, can't help it. Like you, Jeanine, that day in the shop you learned your son was dead. You kept right on working, not saying anything, and everybody else kept quiet, thinking about everybody on the outside, the ones we'd see again, the ones who'd be dead. We all seemed kind of indifferent. I was thinking about you, Dad, backing the car out of the garage the day of my trial, convinced

I'd be acquitted. You're dead now, without my ever having seen you again. Nobody looks at Jeanine. The news circulates through the boxes of lipstick, through the wrappings for the sun visors advertising the Tour de France. Then into the seamstresses' shop, even into the place where they're typing addresses for the telephone books and around the pails and mops of house-keeping, a whispered word on the way to the bathroom and the silence creeps right into the infirmary and the kitchens, silence all morning long in every building. Everybody counting the loved ones who're still alive...

Come on little sister, tell me about your life, your life before this. When you had a name and people called you Ma'am. No. Don't say anything about why or how you got here, tell me about your mother, your brothers, your sister, your kids. Make me laugh little sister. Empty my head of all these gloomy thoughts. Come on. What's your oldest's name? You had a difficult pregnancy and how about your labor, tell me.
How old is he now and how old are you, little sister. Show the beach photos, the communion shots, everything, at every phase. No. It can't be. You mean that little guy there is doing his military service? How about that, you must've started real young. How old were you when he was born? What's your funniest memory? No, not the saddest one, I don't want to hear it. Yeah! the first time you fell in love. It's always like that. It's funny. No kidding! It's just like me. What do you know? Catastrophe's my middle name. Make me laugh, little sister, again and again, until I cry for air and can't go on I'm so bent over from laughing right here in the middle of the cell, and the head guard rushes in and calls us hysterics. Let's laugh. Oh yes let's laugh. Oh that's funny. Oh! Aren't we having a good time. When you're this miserable, you don't have the right to be sad.

"But you can't let them bury your mother like a dog now you're finally free."

"What if I do, it's my mother, it's my life."
"And what about your family, have you thought about them?
Want them to turn their backs on you from the first day you're
out? You really always have been a little wacko, haven't you?"
You know, my family couldn't give a fuck. What matters to them
is the restraining order. I won't bother them for five years.
All those faces at the same time.
No thanks. My aunt and her toilet water. My cousin Pierre
who lost all his clients because of what I did.
All the fuss it caused in the region. My niece whose engage-
ment was broken. Everything that got screwed up is because of
me, you know. She married the village drunk so she wouldn't
become an old maid. A boozy sponge where his brain should
be. And my brother who lost his job when my trial began. They
said something about having to pare down the personnel. It
doesn't matter. He never forgave me. My sister-in-law, depression after depression, first she's paralyzed on the right side,
then on the left. My nephew who was supposed to go to the
best business school in Paris[5] and end up a government minister to make up for all this. He ran off to India. Who knows
where?
So they look at me cross-wise, and say, "Prison isn't like it used
to be, right, I guess they even got television now?"
While serving the wine they saved especially for when I came
home.
"What're you gonna do now? Cuz with what'll be left once your
mother's stuff is split up..." Do you think, Ma'am, that once
your life's been gutted you can stitch it back up as though nothing ever happened? I only had my mother, the rest of the family, forget it, zero.
For sixteen years my life's been here, Ma'am, and now I'm wondering why I'm even leaving. What's out there for me anyway:
kids who're men who don't need me anymore, who knows,
maybe I'll even be a bother to them, my mother's warm corpse,
and two million unemployed workers who'll already have applied

for all the available jobs. There's nothing and nobody. I gave away my things yesterday the way you execute a will. As if I were dead.

Farewell, everybody. Farewell. I ended up loving you. Every one of you. Paulette. You castrated your guy, you did fifteen years, you got out, you castrated another one right away and came back for a second life term. Maybe you found the answer; you're happy, you look after the geraniums in the entrance courtyard. So sweet, so calm. No one would ever believe it.

Véro. You let your son die of hunger in a closet. God knows if we didn't take it out on you. We called you the kid-killer. One day you were cleaning the windows, and you yelled, "So long, old girls," and jumped out. I've often pushed your wheelchair during the exercise period.

And you, Marie-Lou. You found the answer. You talk to your dog. A porcelain dog you got from mail order. A life-sized basset hound. Little by little you baptized your bed, your slippers (you call them the twins), your toothbrush, your house plants, your broom. You don't need anybody any more. You're a lifer too. Sometimes you say, smiling, "You know, I'm not crazy."

And you, The Abominable One, with your solid fat, your swollen face, your little evil pig eyes, you wrote to the President of the Republic, to the Communist Party, to the Pope. You're so ugly. And yet you truly love your girlfriend, and you're so eager to stay in style you buy clothes from all the new arrivals. You found religion here.

Farewell, my dead ones. Neither happy nor unhappy, dead, that's all.

I'm leaving to grab a little real life. I'm going to rinse out my soul. Yes. I'll miss the opened letters they give us with the crossed-out words we try to make out under the x's, the forbidden coffee at 1 a.m., the shop for the down-and-out: "Will you trade me some tobacco for stamps?," the moment when the sleeping pill finally kicks in. The footsteps of the screw at night, the snap of the peephole every two hours, the censured signals, the tap tap tap of the heating pipes.

"What're you doing?"

"I'm saying hello to a friend, Ma'am."

"You can't do that. This isn't the first time we've caught you."

I'll miss my cell where Jean Seberg has walked alone in the rain for sixteen years on a poster facing my bed. Farewell. Yes. I'll always be more from here than from out there. Maybe that's what dies today. I left Nicole my clay pots, with the avocado pits and grapefruit seeds, the sprouting dates—everything took, everything's growing, I've got a green thumb, I listened to the grass grow and the grass watched me live.

Spring, flowers, tussles in bed, love—no, Ma'am, I don't believe in it any more, I'll probably carry around the baggage from here: fat, cavities, badly doctored ulcers, cancer. At the corner bistro, the guys say, "We're better off in this place than across the street." Well maybe I was better off here. My stomach's going crazy. Trying to tell your wandering flesh to relax isn't so easy. Stopping your mind from whirling when the body joins the dance is next to impossible.

Its messages are passed to friendly travelers by radio, books, everpresent transistors—dream faucets.

Imagining love is more painful than its absence. My body cries out. Desire throws itself from the window. I feel like biting my sheets. I listen to the ticking of my blood. Night burns, it's arterial disaster, preparations for the last hour before breaking through the black hole, finally arriving at the other side. Searching in your sleep for the hand you'd like to hold. Screaming in your stone casket from the knowledge of everyone's profound indifference. Breaking all the windows, listening to the echoes reverberate in the big courtyard, feeling the lock of hair on your neck, the last caress left in the world, waking up soaked from the past which has snuck up on you and the anguish which sleeps at the foot of your bed like a curled dog. Wanting to bury yourself in a blank when all your memories start to buzz.

My body is stiff and rigid. The body of a dead woman. In the cell next door, somebody is screaming, "No, no, it wasn't me." Another one having a nightmare. I'm waiting. The easing of dawn. The snap of the peephole one more time. The last sign of human presence. Sweat is drowning my thighs, I'd like to fall down dead, my stomach aches. With all my strength I hug the cold cement floor to feel the earth breathing underneath. Help me. My closed-up cunt is useless, my brain is empty. My ears are filled with sand. My eyes blinder than the Cyclops in the door. Help me. I reach for your hand. You're not there. You're dead. And I killed you. I would've liked to stop myself from doing it. I wasn't really myself. Like a madwoman. But I'm not making excuses. My crime's never left me. Two bullets in the heart. I don't want to cry any more.

I'm forty-nine years old, not quite fifty. I'm ugly now. Since I entered this storage dump, my mind's frittered away. Manoeuvering the last turn isn't easy. I have to break and enter to be enthusiastic again. All my thoughts are darkly racing. And I can almost feel the minute I'll leave this place. I already hear the birds. Am I tough enough? Since I started training myself to gobble up four seasons without breathing, my heart's been hollowed out. Somebody ought to excavate it. I must be bursting at the seams, totally off-base, my sense of humor chipping away. Tell me, what's a man? My box is about to be opened and I'm no gift to anybody.

Morning bells. Already. Have pity on me. I don't want to leave.

Downstage the door opens slowly, releasing a flood of light.

No, I don't want to. A first-class supervisor will come. She'll go with me. My suitcases are waiting at properties. And my pitiful nest egg. And...my identity papers.
Odd seeing a twenty-year-old me on my passport. I'll wear my

suit, it's coming back into style. The skirt's a little long but the jacket's pinched at the waist.

There'll be a white scarf at the window of one of the cells. Nicole's farewell. I won't cry. I'll go through the first set of doors, I'll be in the entrance courtyard, the guard will check my papers one more time and then he'll open wide the swinging doors.
I won't look back, it's bad luck, I'll look straight ahead, at the city. I'm afraid.
Listen to the birds, they're the masters of the world. Listen to the footsteps in the corridor, someone's coming and it's for you. Your door's about to be opened.

Listen to the birds, they're the masters of the world, they bring light to your heart, come on, try, let light into your heart, get up and dance, dance, girl, dance, dance, dance.

> *We see her in shadow as she begins to walk through the door.*
> *Lights dim to black.*

~

TRANSLATOR'S NOTES

In some instances, I have used a more general expression for the specific reference in the French text:

1. "The mail order house" replaces "Les Trois Suisses" (a French mail order house, similar to Sear's).

2. "Social services" replaces DDASS, the acronym for the welfare unit which administers the care of abandoned, abused, or dependent children whose parents cannot care for them.

3. "The Queen of the harem" replaces "Madame Loukoum," a name borrowed from a North African pastry to indicate an "exotic" woman.

4. "An old movie magazine" replaces *Cinémonde*.

5. "The best business school in Paris" replaces the acronym ENA, l'Ecole Nationale d'Administration.

Martine Drai

All It Takes Is
Something
Small

Translated from the French by
Stephen J. Vogel

UBU REPERTORY THEATER PUBLICATIONS
NEW YORK

Martine Drai studied Russian literature in Nice and, at twenty, moved to Paris in order to study acting at the National Conservatory of Dramatic Arts, in the class of Antoine Vitez. Her first part after graduation was in Ibsen's *The Master Builder.* Her novel *Les Trois midis* was published by Le Seuil in 1979. In 1986, Vitez directed her first play, *Alias,* at the Théâtre National de Chaillot. Other writings include the plays *Un amoureux de la vie,* which was given several public readings, and *Lézardes,* which was published under the auspices of the Chartreuse, near Avignon, where she was writer in residence in 1989. In 1993, she was awarded a grant from the Beaumarchais Foundation for the writing of her play *Messe.* Martine Drai has also conducted writing workshops, directed plays and adapted works by Gilles Ben Aych, Italo Calvino and David Garnett. She performed the part of Georgette in the 1994 Paris premiere of *Il suffit de peu,* a production which was partially subsidized by a grant from the Beaumarchais Foundation.

Stephen J. Vogel has previously translated Daniel Besnehard's *Passengers* and *The White Bear,* both published by Ubu, as well as *A Simple Death (Arromanches)* and *The Child in Obock. The White Bear* was produced by Ubu Repertory Theater in 1992. Other translations for Ubu Repertory Theater include *The Prophet and the President* by Jean-Luc Raharimanana (Madagascar), published in *Afrique II, Intelligence Powder* by Kateb Yacine (Algeria), and *The Daughter of the Gods* by Abdou Anta Kâ (Senegal), included in the first *Afrique* anthology now out of print. He is co-translator of Raymond Queneau's *En Passant* presented at the French Institute/Alliance Française as part of Théâtre de la Cabriole's *Be-Bop at Saint-Germain-des-Prés.*

AUTHOR'S NOTE

In a small, provincial train station, late in the afternoon, an old woman is talking.

She's a "bag lady," and not unaware of how other people view her. Their reactions amuse her, and furnish a subject for her rambling discussions with those who observe her, the passengers arriving, or waiting for a train. Her conversations touch upon the constraints imposed by their hectic lives, anxious and over-structured.

She talks of herself, as well. She tells her own story. She reveals how she came to her present situation: it all started with a dream. A simple dream, recurring every night, one which turned her life upside down. It was a dream about a coat.

A beautiful coat. Gray. A gray beyond all imagining, surpassing every hope.

Possibly, she's lying. Possibly, she's making the whole thing up. The coat and all the rest of it. For she has more than one tale to tell.

It's also possible she's telling the truth.

And no matter how long she goes on talking, no one will ever know for sure.

MARTINE DRAI

PRODUCTION NOTES

Georgette, the woman speaking, is dressed so outlandishly that it's impossible to make out the shape of her body .

Her face, too, is almost hidden by locks of hair, a cap, a hat and one or more scarfs.

And then there are various objects, sticking out of her pockets, attached to her belt, etc.

Near her is a tote bag. Inside, a bottle.

The people that she talks to may be presented on stage or not, as desired.

The actress playing this part need not, in actual fact, be very old.

I still have my last ID.
You can't see the date of birth anymore.
A big gob of tar on it.
Don't know how that could've happened.
But lots of things you don't know how they happened.
'Cause I never had to show my ID card.
Almost never. Right. Sure, I got hassled like everybody else.
Oh yeah, I got hassled. But not as much as I thought. 'Cause I
thought I was gonna get hassled a lot more. When you come
right down to it, it was a piece of cake. You live a hundred years,
piece of cake. A hundred years or more. Nobody'll ever know
my age, with that gob of tar. One morning they'll find me dead,
they'll go through my bag there. They'll see the photo on my
card, they'll wonder how I could've changed so much. That'll
keep 'em busy. They'll never find that out, my age.

Boy, how I walked, from the time I left. Maybe ten thousand
kilometers. Or fifteen, or twenty-five thousand, who knows, I
wasn't counting.
Before, I did, I counted. Before I left.
I lived in Paris. Fourteenth Arrondissement. A cute little apartment. I had one. Yeah, just like you. A sixth-floor walkup. When
I left I was already almost old but I could still get up and
down those six flights, no trouble. I had good legs. Beautiful,
too. That's what they used to say. Georgette has such beautiful legs. Georgette's my name. I don't like it, never have.
I learned to live with it. Like you did with yours. We've all been
there, right? It's true I had beautiful legs. Not even the men
in my life liked 'em as much as I did. They never caught on.
Men never catch on how nice it is to look good to yourself.
That's their problem. Or maybe not. They're happier when
they don't catch on.

I call these my saviors.

Could look at 'em for hours.

I call them my saviors 'cause I found them in the garbage on Christmas night.

When there's nobody around here, sometimes I talk to them. I tell them they're my saviors. I sure hope you're my last pair. I'm fed up with walking. After you, that's it.

'Cause there's nobody around this station at night. That's why I like the big stations better.

The station master here, he puts on his cap five minutes before the train comes in, and takes it off soon as it pulls out. That's the way it is in these little stations.

You're wondering why I'm talking to you. You're about to catch your train and you're saying to yourself, what's this crazy lady want with me? I'll tell you: I like people who wait for trains. 'Cause I used to wait, too. We've all been there, right, waiting. But now I don't wait anymore. You do. You remind me of me, before.

Pretty soon it'll be here again, Christmas. Those lighted things all over. They stick that stuff up over your head and never ask what you think and...

Well, people got to have fun, sure. But is that really fun, that's my question. All's I got to do now is ask myself questions. I'm taking advantage, see. Before I was like you, no time.

Sure they're too big for me. I hear what goes on in your head. Well, that's exactly what made me take them, see. 'Cause in winter it's better if you have more room for your feet. I've always thought my feet were very important. Feet and legs, it's all built on them.

I was a real beauty. You can't really tell now, but I was. A knock-out. Elegant, in fact. It goes with the territory, you'll see what

I mean. So when I left, I got a kick out of seeing myself go
through all the changes. I tell you, buddy, you see your skin get
hard. Well, leather gets thick. And then your mouth. It starts
to change shape. When your teeth go, your mouth gets all
sucked in. Then there's the hair. You don't brush it you don't
wash it anymore. So you end up with dog fur on your head.
My hair meant a lot to me. I kept it long all my life. Coco Chanel
and Jean Seberg? Who cares! The latest styles didn't impress
me. At least not that kind. 'Cause when it came to the other
kind, that was my territory, see. But as for my hair, I kept it long
right up to the end. Almost to the end. 'Til the day I met him,
the guy. The loony. The Englishman. It's because of him that
I cut it. Now wait, I'm not saying that I'm sorry. He made me
laugh, that Englishman. And I hadn't laughed in a dog's age.
I don't smell, you know. You can come closer.
Okay, I smell a little. Just a little. It won't kill you.
What's his problem? I know what goes through people's heads.
So what if I smell. You think you don't smell? Sometimes. Oh,
but that's just in private, your smells. Well, you see, with me
it's in public. And what's the big difference? You tell me.

But the day you start to smell bad, that you never forget.
A dirty old woman, boy, that's what you smell like!
Just being old you smell bad. Even when you're clean, if you're
old you smell bad. So why should I bother to stay clean. See,
one day, there was this girl, real young, and she looks down at
me, all the way down from her Chanel Number 19, well I used
to wear Chanel Number 19, too, and now I think it stinks, you
see what it means to evolve, so anyway, the girl looks at you and
she starts to wonder, about things connected to the feminine
condition, if you catch my drift, feminine hygiene, get it? But
you don't give a shit about her. 'Cause all the questions that
girl's asking herself, they're all beside the point. 'Cause you're
not really a woman any more. She should've caught on right
away, that girl.

He doesn't know what to say to me. Completely stumped.
Don't worry, I don't want you to say anything. It wouldn't matter if I did, nobody ever says anything to me. That's how it is. I'm the woman nobody ever says anything to, that's what I'm here for.
Your train's gonna get in, and I'll be all alone again. But later, I'll go on with someone else. I'm used to it. I don't really care, to tell you the truth. Don't worry about it.

I left everything, my whole life up till then, because of this coat. This one, right. All it takes is something small. This was small. And that's all it took.
You see this coat. It started out gorgeous. So gorgeous that I can't even describe it.
It lost all its color in the wars. Everything stuck to it, all kinds of shit, same as to me, that's what it's here for, it's a good companion, a companion in arms, take a good look at it and respect it, I say. It's stood up to everything. Dust, mud, tar that melts in the summer, snow, rain. It's served me well. It's protected me as much as it could. But it's gotten thinner. Like me. So, I gave it some help. That's why you see me covered up like this. All alone, it couldn't do it. In fact, to tell you the truth, it's not much good anymore. But I'll hold on to it right to the end. 'Cause it's been good. And what's more, this coat is my conscience, as you're gonna see, whaddya think, you think you just throw your conscience away, like that?

Don't think I didn't keep myself clean at first. At first, you do keep yourself clean. That's what public showers are for. The thing is, little by little I got tired of it. The rot sets in, you just give up. There's a pleasure in that, believe it or not. You let yourself go and it's a pleasure. I may look like a loony but I ponder these things, I take the time, yes. And when you ponder you notice the subtleties.

Well anyway, I could keep myself clean if I wanted to. I can still afford a trip to the bathhouse. Only let's be honest, think about it. You see all these duds I'm carrying around on me. If I want to get clean, I've got to take 'em off. And once I get washed I'm gonna have to put them back on. 'Cause I get cold, I'm cold all the time, that's why I've got so much on in the first place. And in the stalls at the bathhouse, there's no room to put all this stuff down the way you'd like to. So that kind of discourages me. And that's why I don't keep myself clean. I used to keep clean up until the cold got to me and—

I'm sure you've never been inside a bathhouse. You ought to try it sometime, it's not so bad. You get undressed in all the steam that comes from other people, the walls are thin, you share all the body odors. And you hear all the sounds of the water. And the other sounds. You wouldn't believe how many men there are who jerk off in the shower. I swear to God.
There he goes. He thinks I'm about to launch into a whole series of horror stories. Well, he's wrong, I'll stop right there. And anyway, it's not so horrible. At least, I don't think so. When I hear a man jerking off, I find it kind of touching. Really. A worthy effort. Always a worthy effort. Mustn't belittle a person's efforts. Ever.
That's right, run and catch your train, run along...

I want to die in a train station. But I'd rather it was a big one, not here. In the big ones people can jostle each other better. And the noise. The noise under the windows overhead. The bigger the place is, the more you feel like you're in a swimming pool.
This station master is off his rocker. Some day I'm going to tell him. Hey, couldn't you keep your cap on for just five minutes more?
It's not that I don't like people who work for the railroads. I do. You see 'em with their trains, you can tell they mean a lot

to them. They treat 'em like their own kids, their trains. But I wouldn't like to die here. Station's too small.

So why do I stay here?

It's 'cause of the picture.

The picture over there, next to the door to the restrooms. It's a bird's-eye view of the station. With everything, every detail. The tracks, the crossings, the switch tower, the buildings. There are pictures like that in every train station. But that one is my real favorite. When you see the picture from way back, it's shaped like a fish. A long fish. Like a pike or a mackerel. And the glass covering the picture is cracked. They haven't replaced it yet. It must have gotten cracked a real long time ago. So anyway, you see this crack, well it makes a line, and this line—this is fantastic—this line goes all the way down Track A, and right at the end it veers off, but just a little, and it's all moldy inside, it's gotten brown and green with age, that's what makes Track A look like... I don't know exactly, some kind of underwater landscape, see, with some really weird-looking fungus...

Well, I'm staying here because of that. I like that picture with the broken glass covering it. But when they finally get around to replacing the glass, maybe then I'll go.

Which means that maybe I'll never go.

When you come right down to it, I don't really care.

I don't really care if I go or not. I'll go when I feel like it. Nothing's holding me here.

You're waiting for the 5:56?

Obviously. Otherwise why would you be here? Not just to look at my beautiful eyes, that's for sure. You won't believe it, but they were. Beautiful.

It's going to be late, that train of yours. It always is, the 5:56. Not by much, but always. Two-three minutes. Seventeen, that was the most. Always late. Who knows why it is. Lots of things you don't know why it is.

It's going to be late and you're early. And not just a little bit, either.

So I'm going to give you a little treat. To make the time pass. I'm going to tell you how I got here. Yes. 'Cause that's what you're wondering. Everybody wants to know that, it's only natural.

Here's the story: I used to work in the high fashion industry. Finishing and trimming garments were my areas of expertise. Forty-one years I spent bent over some other dame's glad rags. You could pay six months rent with the price of one of those dresses. And I'm only talkin' bottom of the line, too. Forty-one years. Apprentice at fifteen, I worked my way up, slowly, patiently. I was patient alright. A lifetime of patience. Like you. Like everybody. Just to live you need a helluva lot of patience. We've all been there, right?

Forty-one years. Without once understanding the first thing about my dumb little life. Until one day.

Wait, this all started with a dream. You'll see what I mean.

One night I dreamed about a coat. A gray coat. I never dream in color, not me.

The next morning I remember the dream. And the coat.

The next night, the same dream. And there's the coat, the same coat.

And the same thing every night. By now I can't get that coat out of my mind. I know it by heart. I've got it right there, in my eyes, in my hands, on my skin. It got so I knew it so well that I began to really start looking for it, it was all I could think about, I'd go through the fashion magazines with a fine-tooth comb, I went around to all the clothing stores...and I came up empty-handed. Every night that same dream again, and every day I went out looking...until the time came when I had to tell myself take it easy, Georgette, it's only a dream, and a dream is something you don't find in real life.

And guess what? I was wrong.

I did find it.

And you know how I found it?

At that second-hand place, Emmaüs', one Sunday afternoon. I went with one of my girlfriends, she'd just gotten married, well she needed everything and at rock-bottom prices. Shelves, lamps, dishes, linens, etc. After a couple of hours elbowing our way through the place, it was like this big airplane hangar, and cold, it's a good thing we were running around so much, she says that's enough, Georgette, let's call it quits, I think I've got enough to last till my Golden Wedding Anniversary, at least. We were broke but we were laughing our heads off, all legs and no brains you might say. Well, to make a long story short, she goes to the nearest register to pay. Twenty-five people in line. I see she's gotta wait so I go off to have a look at the old clothes bins. So right away you see I wasn't in my usual state of mind. 'Cause as a rule I wasn't really into old clothes in those days. I only liked new stuff, the *crème de la crème*. Goes with the territory.

Anyhow, I get to these bins and I stick both my hands into one of 'em. And I feel with my fingers this fabric...soft, so soft... I pull on it, it comes up... And all at once I recognize it. It's my dream coat.

It wasn't old. Dusty, sure, and down the front this big long stain all raggedy around the edges, looked like an island kinda. But it wasn't old.

In fact when I went up to the register to buy it they said to me, there's some mistake, it got into that bin by mistake, you can see for yourself, why it's brand new, that'll be an extra fifty francs. Needless to say, I forked over those fifty francs without batting an eye.

Next day I took it to the dry cleaner's. They said it would take a week. The usual. The thing was, I wouldn't go along with it. I felt ripped off, see, I didn't want to let go of it for that long, not that coat. We went on and on about it, finally they gave in, okay, they go, four days, but not one day sooner.

I was shaking when I left the cleaner's. My cheeks were burning, I had this kind of fever. I really thought they were going to lose it. And you know what? The funny thing is, I felt like I would be losing it for the second time.

That's twice in less than a minute you've looked at your watch. It's 7 to, and your train is gonna be late. No thank you, I don't want any money. That knocks you for a loop, right, somebody like me who won't take money. I'm talking to you, listen to me, that's all I need, for now. I'm richer than you are. Really.

So, four days later I go back, and they give me back my coat That islandy-looking stain, gone. Completely. I run home, I double lock my door. Usually, I only lock it around midnight, before I go to bed, and just the upper lock, once. Sometimes I completely forget.

Right at that moment, I didn't pay much attention. It was only later that I remembered it. A long time after, that I locked both locks. And I think about that simple action all the time now.

I don't know. Maybe it's the same for everybody. We remember two-three actions we performed in our lives, that's all, but all the time we remember.

But back then, they meant nothing.

I was at home, nobody around to see me. I took off all the wrapping from the dry cleaner's. I looked at the coat. I'd never looked at anything before the way I looked at that coat, just then. I fondled it, I turned it over and over. From the stitching around the arm-holes and the lining, you could tell it was brand new, the silk wasn't the least bit worn. It was new and it was mine. And that color. That gray. You can't see anything of that gray now. It was an intelligent sort of gray, changeable, it went from greenish-gray to blue gray and then dappled, hot or cold, depending on the light and how it fell on it and all on account of the material. A cloth coat, yes. But the kind of cloth they don't make nowadays, I'm sure of that. I'm out of the business but I know what's out there, on the market. It was a supple kind of cloth, soft and velvety, and at the same time it hung perfectly, a clean, straight drop. The way fine material should hang.

It buttoned like a man's coat.

Yes.

But other than that it went way beyond fashion, and way beyond male or female. And I knew it would be too big for me but that I would feel comfortable in it. And warm.

But that first night, I didn't try it on. I was in no hurry. I fondled it, and turned it over and over, laid it on my lap and then I hung it in my closet. Between a lamé dress, I'll have more to say about that dress, I always have more to say about that dress— Between that lamé dress and my chinchilla. My fake chinchilla. Carven style.

I wore fakes during the whole first part of my life. Forty-one years of fakes. A kind of walking imitation, that was me. It's because of the coat that I became conscious of the fact. There's your train. Bon voyage.

I put it in my closet and didn't look at it again all evening.

The next morning I get to the workroom five minutes late. Lucky for me my supervisor didn't say anything about it. But I decided then and there I'd better mind my P's and Q's for the rest of the day...but right in the middle of the afternoon I start to think of that coat again. It was like a fly buzzing around me, the thought of that coat. Now a fly is nothing much, but *it* makes the decision when to leave *you* alone, and not the other way around. I see it all as if it were yesterday. That afternoon I was stuck with seventy-five meters of silver sequins that had to be sewn to the hem of a crepe de Chine dress in veronese green. Even today, all I have to do is shut my eyes and remember that shade of green and I get nauseous. I was bent over my work, and thinking of the coat. And then something funny flashed in front of my eyes, getting all mixed up with the thread, and the sequins and the green. I saw all of the clothes hanging in my closet parading past me, against that shade of green. And just when the coat appeared, the parade came to a sudden halt.

It was enough to make my head spin. And my fever came back. After a moment I couldn't take it any more, so I got up and went to see the supervisor and I told her I can't take it any more, it's my eyes, I can't see clearly, a bad headache, I feel like throwing up, I've gotta get out of here... Well, she looks down her nose at me, then she says by all means, leave, Georgette, but don't let this happen again... You realize, my dear, if everyone carried on like you...

So. That's it. That's how it all began. I walked back to my place instead of taking the metro. Two hours on foot. I had to do it. I felt like the wind was knocked out of me, that's how mad I was. I had to get my wind back, so I walked. 'Cause it was the first time in my life I ever asked to leave the workroom early. You realize, my dear, if everyone carried on like you... It knocked me for a loop. And at 56 years of age I began to understand where I was. And who I was. A poor fool. And all too happy to dress like those rich old biddies.

I went by the Luxembourg. I looked at the things around me, it was almost like I didn't know them any more. Nothing. The Medici Fountain, the kiosque, the refreshment stand, the statues, the poneys, the tennis court, nothing, I wasn't part of it any more, I was no longer in a place I knew.

Once I was back in my neighborhood, I didn't go up to my apartment right away. I went to sit down in a cafe. I asked for a glass of wine, then a second, then a third... I used to drink only on special occasions, before... But after that I never stopped. And I'm not sorry. And all that I owe to the coat.

'Cause the next day, I didn't go back to the workroom. And never again after that.

When you begin to understand certain things, you can't stop yourself. So I had the feeling that I was able to breathe for the first time in my life. I unplugged my phone and I've never plugged it in since.

I walked through Paris and looked around me. And everywhere it was the same as at the Luxembourg, I wasn't part of it any

more, in Paris. Something had broken down. I had to go somewhere else.

So I left.

God, it was hard to pack two suitcases, and no more. I spent
hours standing in my closet. Looking at what was left. Well, I
hadda dress myself, I couldn't just throw it all out.

 I can still see them, as if I was still there.

The fake chinchilla, Carven style.

A very old light-blue cotton dress that I kept from when I was
young...

A light mauve and purple checked wool dress...

A gold lamé jersey sheath, I'll have more to say about it, I always
have more to say about it...

The Asphodel model, the fake Asphodel model... A full bias-
cut cream-colored silk number with a taffeta rosette on the hip...

And I could go on like that for an hour without stopping, that's
how many dresses I had. And where would that get us, in the end?

I used to love my work. I knew all the fabrics, it was like I'd
invented them. With my eyes closed, just by the smell, I could
tell a cotton from a silk, a crepe from a wool. Yes. I wonder if I
could still do it. It's hard to believe you could love your work
so much and then, wham, just like that, give it up, like having
your arm cut off.

I'm sticking with this coat. I'll stick with it right up to the end.
'Cause it was able to show me what it wanted.

I was standing in my closet that morning looking for something
to wear, I couldn't even dress myself properly at that point...
when all at once I saw it rise up from the shelf above, where I
had put it, and it pounced on me so it got dark in the closet...
it was like, I don't know, like an eclipse...night came on without any warning...and I felt it squeezing me, it was squeezing
me so hard I was suffocating, it didn't want me to go to work,
I struggled... I don't know how long I was struggling...or how

long it stayed dark...it's done that every time I—

I left and went to the Southwest. A little out-of-the-way place,
very quiet. I knew it very well, I'd been there twice before, on
vacations. Two weeks each time. My paid vacations. I used to
have paid vacations, too, you know. I stayed in the same hotel.
A quiet little hotel, and the rooms smelled of vervain, that was
the perfume the chambermaid used.
A little out-of-the-way place near Bordeaux. Sort of inland.
But there was this lake. Not far away. Not far for me, two hours
on foot, I've never minded walking.
It stops in the station for three minutes, no need to rush like
that. It's crazy how scared people get. It's all out of proportion.
They're scared of missing their train, as if, I don't know...
Or else, who knows, maybe they're afraid of not missing it.
People are hard to figure.

The smell of vervain. It stayed with me all the while I was spending what little savings I had.
I left it all behind me in that little place. Forty-one years'
worth of savings. Everything went in just two seasons. When I
got there it was spring and when I got out winter was just starting. I was in a hurry to see it go, I mean the money I saved. It
represented my whole life as a stupid fool.

She's here without her book today.
On time, though. At the usual time for her. 6:35 p.m., and here
she is.
So why didn't you bring your book today?
And why are you always on the platform across from me? Do I
scare you? Or maybe it's so you can watch me better?
If you came over on my platform, you could hear me better. I
can't shout, my voice is too weak. It's not a question of my age.
Not exactly. I never had what you'd call an opera singer's voice.
Too bad for you. Stay where you are. You'll just have to hear as

best you can.

But it's too bad you don't have your book today. 'Cause I really like it when you read. You remind me of when I was young. Boy, I used to read a lot. A little of everything. That's how I educated myself culturally. You might say.

When you read, it looks like you're dreaming. Your eyes half-closed darting around.

Men, when they dream, they look like dogs.

But a dog will always look like he's dreaming more than a man. Nobody knows why, but that's the way it is.

How come you always come here at the same time?

Is this the time you get out of work?

She won't answer.

Okay. She comes to the station to clear her head. It's true, everything is new at a train station. We're alike, you see, we both like train stations. I'd like to die in a station. But not this one, it's too small.

Did you notice the picture that looks like a fish? Over there by the restrooms? No, I guess not, since you're so attached to your platform across the way. Well, maybe you had your own routine, even before I got here.

When you go back to the same place every day to find something you like, it's a little like having your own house.

Now, mind you, it's not that I want my own house, ya know...

You gotta watch out for houses.

Houses are dangerous places.

You should go and see that picture. It's nice.

And under the picture there's a notice posted that's interesting, too. Sometimes at night before I fall asleep I say it over to myself. I know it by heart now. Memory, that's important. Gotta exercise your memory. Memory is like a muscle. Required routes for all employees assigned to travel to and from offices signal posts locomotive shops or switch yards. For their own safety those employees whose duties require travel between offices signal posts locomotive shops or switch yards are obliged to follow only those routes indicated on the above map by a black line, either solid for cycle traffic, or dotted for non-cycle traffic. In the case of those routes allowing for cycle traffic in one direction only, employees must follow the direction indicated by the arrows. New paragraph. When traveling alone or in groups along designated routes, employees are required to observe those precautions designed to insure the personal safety of each individual and especially those precautions indicated by Rule Number P9 regarding the safety of all personnel.

You noticed that memory, right? And at my age, too. All brains and no legs, these days. Just the opposite from when I was young. And it's all because I exercise it. A person's intelligence is half memory. I read that in a magazine. I don't read books any more but I still read magazines. There are plenty of 'em around in a train station. It's the people getting off the trains who leave 'em behind.
There are more people getting on than people getting off here. It doesn't make sense but that's how it is.

The last books I read were at the lake. Yes. That's when it stopped.

Mornings at my little hotel, soon as I'd get out of bed, my mind would be racked with questions. Such as maybe I oughta see if I can collect on my pension fund, is the landlady mad at me 'cause I didn't give her any notice, is my mail going to be opened and by who, are my sister and my nephews going to worry too much. And will they have put out a missing persons bulletin on me?
Oh, I had a family. Like you. And friends. I had everything you have. I had everything that everybody has. And then all at once I left everything behind. It's true.
Every time I went into town to draw out some cash, I expected

to see my face on a poster, my photo pinned up somewhere. And every morning when I woke up my brain would be pounding. But soon as I started walking, soon as I headed toward the lake, and especially when I got there, poof, all gone. I loved that lake. I forgot about everything when I was in front of it. Everything. The pension fund, the landlady, the family, everything. All I hadda do was look at that lake and it swallowed everything up, it washed me clean of everything.

And when I think back on it now, as far as that missing persons bulletin goes, I was wrong to get worried about it. 'Cause I've always been scared of cameras. And the only pictures of me that they could've come up with were so old nobody woulda recognized me.

In those days, I used to dine like a queen. I had my own table in a de luxe restaurant right down by the lake. Every single day, honey. And every single day, I'd pay a bill that totaled one quarter of what I used to earn in a month. I was in a hurry. My life's savings burned a hole in my pocket. In that restaurant I drank bottles of wine, like never before and never since. And I tasted dishes the like of which I couldn't have begun to imagine. With names I couldn't have imagined, either.

At the end of the summer, that was it, my finances went into the red. But I stayed at the hotel. Delighted to be able to write them a rubber check.
The first rubber check I'd ever written in my whole life as a stupid fool.
I sold the jewelry I'd inherited from my family to get some cash. It didn't bring me much. You know, with that kind of jewelry, you love it, you think it's worth a lot, and then the jewelers go and tell you it's not worth a thing. You take it as best you can. So, I decided to keep a topaz ring. I kept it right up to the day I happened to meet the Englishman.

But I'm not sorry. That Englishman made me laugh, I hadn't laughed in the longest time.

In those days at the lake, I was what they call a belle. Embellished. Fine wines, good food, fresh air, never had I looked so lovely. And yet, when you come down to it, I didn't have a single man during that whole time. I enjoyed looking at myself in the nude, but my mind wasn't on sex. Everything was focused on the lake. I watched the trees change, and the water changed, too, faster, every day, every minute, I savored my time there, that was enough for me. I wanted that time all for myself.

Sometimes I try to recall the last man I had.
When I was a kid, I used to think to myself: an old lady must remember her last man...
But try as I might, I just can't. It's the first one you remember. The first one who counts, I mean. And God knows it may be a long time before he comes along.

I walked out of the hotel one night, around mid-November. Left a rubber check on the front desk and the next morning I took a bus to another little place, about a hundred kilometers from there.

At first I lugged 'em around with me, my two suitcases. I couldn't get rid of them. That was when I got into the habit of sleeping in train stations. And see, that's why I like the big ones better. They don't shut down at night. Course, here they're nice. They shut down but they let me stay inside. In the waiting room. They know that I'm cold. I'm always cold. That's the reason I keep myself so bundled up.

I've never gone up to Paris again. And I never will, either. By now I know there's nothing to worry about, nobody would recognize me. But at first that was the only thing on my mind. I could just see my best friend's face, say, if she recognized me.

And it's not like I'm ashamed or anything. No, what it is is that when people are so nice to you you can't say no. You don't say no, 'cause you want to please them, so you just step back in line.

Boy was I cold, that first winter. It was a wicked winter, even there—I was still down south. Maybe it was starting that winter that I've never been able to get warm.
No, wait, once, and only that one time, I got warm. When I met him, the guy.
The loony, the Englishman. It's true.

It was at the end of that first winter that I got rid of one of my two suitcases.
It was lunch time, all around me was a mingling of smells, from the kitchen and the mimosa, oh they were gorgeous that year, I was walking down a little street and all of a sudden I looked to the end of a courtyard and saw a house, three stories tall, with a banner strung across the top floor saying: "Companions of Emmaüs". I said to myself it's now or never, and I left one of my two suitcases in that courtyard.

Last night I had a dream. And since this morning I've been going over it in my mind, it keeps me company.
It's not that it's so cheerful. Not cheerful, not sad.

See, first there were my feet. In front of me there was someone who was fitting me with shoes. I've always thought my feet were very important. I couldn't see the head of the person on their knees in front of me. Only the hands. They were big, red, pudgy hands. Not a man's, not a woman's. I couldn't tell. And a voice tells me they look so good on you, my how good they look on you...
And then a big nothing, a whiteout. Or a blackout, I don't know.
Well, there was a cutaway, like in the movies.
After that I saw myself at home, in my apartment in the Fourteenth Arrondissement. I saw myself in bed. I saw myself and at the

same time I was actually there, sound asleep. But all of a sudden, I woke up, all sweaty, well, it was like when you'd wake up during the war feeling panicky, but this wasn't the war any more, there was absolutely nothing, just a woman sitting with her back to me at the foot of my bed, and I said to her they're waiting for me! They're waiting for me at the shoe store! I have an appointment at eight o'clock! I'm late!... But the woman sitting there didn't want to turn around. Or maybe she couldn't. Well anyway, I got up, I started to run, I didn't look at her again, I dashed like crazy through the streets, but always there were more streets. And when I got to the shoe store, I saw a clock floating before me, over a sign shaped like a lace-up boot, and it read "8:25". And pressed up against the store window, the face of my co-worker at the workroom, and she was banging that pair of shoes against the window. And she was shouting my how good they look on you, my how good they look on you... Then I saw myself there, I saw myself as if I was her, on the other side of the window, and I was wearing the gold lamé dress I wore for the last time on the day I met him. The guy. The loony.

There's no reason to feel sorry for me.
I made a lot today. I'm richer than you are.
342 francs and 60 centimes, plus an Italian token. They have the nerve to give me centimes, or foreign coins. Doesn't faze 'em a bit.
But I was able to afford my favorite whisky. It's there, in my bag. I'm waiting till it's night to open it.
It was the Englishman who gave me that. That whisky. Before him, I didn't know anything about it. It's a special kind of whisky. At least I can say he left me that. It's better than nothing.

Every night it gets dark a little sooner. Well, face it, autumn's here. I'm going to get colder and colder.
They turn back the clock on Sunday. Monday, when you come here to read at 6:35, there'll only be the electric light. What's more, you forget your glasses half the time, I've noticed.

She's going. Of course, it's time for her to do that.
Till tomorrow, maybe. Maybe I'll still be here. As long as they
haven't replaced the glass I'll be here.
After that, we'll see.

Poor guy. Poor slob.
But I did get my whisky. He counted it out, all in coins, that 297
francs and 35 centimes. I pitied him, really, in that pretty shop
of his, with his white burgundies at 500 francs a bottle. I felt
sorry for him, seeing him counting like that. He was counting
like I had, ten minutes before. With the money in his hand.
See, when you panhandle for a living, that's the only way you
count. Numbers don't exist any more.
I used to really like numbers, when I was still living like an idiot.
I used to do my calculations. I could've been an accountant.
Numbers are beautiful things.

But anyway I got my whisky. See this bottle, it's the most beautiful bottle that I know. 'Cause it doesn't look like a whisky
bottle. It looks more like a wine bottle. You see the label, very
plain. A bottle of vintage wine. That's what I like, when things
are different from the way they look. That's why I like this whisky.

I saw him from far away, that Englishman, way before he saw
me. I was sitting in front of one of those gigantic shopping cen-
ters, a Mammoth, I think it was, or one of 'em like a Mammoth.
One Saturday afternoon. I was thinking to myself with all those
shoppers, that's where the money'll be. Well, guess what? Fat
chance. People are so stingy when they're in a hurry to do their
weekly shopping. Stingy, you have no idea. I sat there watching
all those stingy people, and feeling bored to death... When all
of a sudden, out of the corner of my eye, I see a kind of fire...
I turn my head, and there he is.
The sun shining on his hair.
He was strawberry blond. With his skin covered with freckles.

But I only found that out later...

For the moment, I'm still far away from him...and what really catches my eye is that underneath the hair I see this cardboard box, but what a box. Huge. He was carrying it in his arms, it was throwing him off balance, he was almost falling over every step he took, I said to myself, Jesus H. Christ, what's with that weirdo, can't he use a shopping cart like everybody else?

Looking back now, what seems weird to me is that the machine inside the box, it's one I didn't think you could buy in a big shopping center. But maybe I'm not in the know any more when it come to things like that. Like what you can and what you can't buy in a shopping center, like Mammoth. Like Mammoth and big ones.

When he got to the parking lot, he set down the box for a moment to look for his car. That was when I noticed that firstly he was a good-looking kid, and secondly he was dressed like somebody pretty upper class. Three-piece suit, simple but elegant, and shoes to die for... A light bulb went on over my head, I got up. Georgette, I said to myself, this guy will make up for all the others...

He starts on his way, I tail him right behind. We go a whole kilometer through the parking lot till we get to his car, I check out the English license plate, he sets the box down, looks me over from head to toe, he says to me what do you want?

A charming little accent.

I answer back a hundred francs, a hundred franc bill would be a big help.

He smiles, scratches his chin, scratches the side of his nose, nods his head, he opens the trunk of his car, tries to put the box inside, this way, that way, it doesn't fit, he decides to put it on the back seat, all the while looking like he's thinking about something and ignoring me at the same time, and finally he makes me his offer. What it is is he has the hundred francs, see, no problem there, and I can have the money, but there's a catch. I've gotta do him a little favor. A kind of job, but no difficulty involved so he says.

Uh-oh, I say to myself, a kind of job, watch your step, Georgette. I ask him for further information. Which he supplies. I accept. He says to me, well, since we're in agreement I'll come pick you up here late this afternoon. I say to him be more specific, okay, I'm a very busy person. He specifies. Then he takes off.

It was then early afternoon. It was hot outside. It was autumn, but the sun had been beating down all morning like we were right in the middle of August. Like I already said, I know I repeat myself but that's how it is with words, there are some you can't find and there are some you can't get rid of, like I said before I'm cold all the time, all the time, ever since I left. But that day, when I met him, I don't know how it happened, but I felt the heat. Felt it like never before.

It got to the point where I had to take off a few layers. Only thing was, I wasn't about to do it out in the parking lot, for sure. I took my suitcase and my tote bag and I went into the Mammoth, looking for the restrooms. They charge you two francs just to pee, but I had the money and I paid, I hate paying for nothing, anyway once inside I was able to get undressed without too much trouble. And all of a sudden, in the middle of getting undressed, I don't know what came over me, I said to myself Georgette, how about sprucing up a little for that weirdo Englishman...

And out of my suitcase I took my gold lamé sheath. And I slipped it on. All the while keeping a pair of slacks and a little sweater on underneath, and my coat on over it. You should never be too exposed, 'cause that could cause a bad case of congestion. Anyway. I put everything back in the suitcase, and I go sit down again in front of the entrance to the shopping center. I was pretty pleased at the thought of seeing the Englishman again, I said to myself, Georgette, baby, you haven't spoken English since the war, this'll take you back to the days of your youth.

'Cause I had a kind of adventure, that I did, learning English. An amorous adventure, needless to say. But beautiful. However,

I'm keeping the details to myself.

Say, you couldn't spare me a cigarette, by any chance, long as you got 'em out?
Thanks.

These cigarettes of yours are good. Reminds me of the ones we used to smoke all the time, me and the other girls in the workroom, way back when. I don't remember who it was put us on to them. Palettes, they were called. Super-thin box and a different color for each cigarette. Also, they tasted of honey. They went off the market around the middle of the 60's. Right during the Courrèges period. A real glut on the market, Courrèges. Okay, so maybe I'm exaggerating a bit, but back then you couldn't escape that look. A fashion disaster on a global scale.
I wonder why they stopped making them, those Palettes.
Things come and they go. Like people.

He came back just when he said. 6:30 on the dot, there he was, in front of me in the parking lot. I sat in the passenger's seat, he stuck my suitcase in the trunk, I kept my tote bag on my lap. The whole ride, not one word. He had a sour look on his face. Must have thought I smelled. Not even a nice word for my gold lamé dress. There are some things men say and some they don't. And not just men.
A sour look on his face. Or else he was concentrating. Anyway, complete silence till we got on this kind of rocky dirt road with all these twists and turns and going up, way up. On the way he went over the main part of his plan again, namely that I was supposed to attend this tennis match of his, and the match was gonna have two parts, see, a first part where he was gonna use the machine, the machine that was in the box, and a second part where he was gonna be alone without anything. A tight little smile on the alone without anything. At the time I didn't

pay any attention to that smile. It was only later that it came back to me. Much later, obviously.

Finally he wound up by telling me again what he said before, that I only had to watch him, but that in order to watch him I'd have to agree to climb up on the umpire's chair.

Well, I told him, okay, no problem.

I'd never climbed up on an umpire's chair before, it was kind of a break from my usual routine.

So we get up to the top of the hill, he stops the car right in front of the entrance to the tennis court. We get out. He takes the box from off the back seat, I tell him I want my suitcase. He says you don't need your suitcase to watch me play. I tell him I need it for my psychological satisfaction. That caught him off guard, so he gets out my suitcase. We get out, we get to the court, he points out the umpire's chair.

Ouch, I go, you didn't tell me that this was a freak chair.

What's freakish about it? he says.

Well, don't you see? Don't you see it's too high?

That's what happens when you drink too much, he tells me, it looks taller to you than it really is.

I'm not going up there, I tell him, I don't wanna break my neck.

If you don't climb up there, you won't get a thing out of me. You've got to watch me from on top of the chair. Those are the terms of our agreement. It's either that or nothing.

And he sets down my suitcase, goes back to the car to get his gym bag, goes into the locker room, leaving me standing there. Faced with a moral dilemma.

Well. I was baffled for a while, then I did what anybody in my situation would have done: I plunked my suitcase down on one of the seats in the stands, I put my bag down at the foot of that chair from hell, I swallowed what was left of the wine in my bottle, not much I might add, and I put my foot on the first rung. All I hadda do was continue. I worked up my courage looking at the beauty of the late afternoon. An autumn light, see, golden, something like today, and the white of the chair stood out against

the dark green of all the shrubbery around the court...it was
real nice. Real nice.

I'd just put my foot on the third rung when I saw the nutcase
come out of the locker room dressed for action. I've got to
say, that white outfit looked very nice on him. A good-looking
kid. The tall, wiry kind. I've always liked that. And there I was
admiring him, like the nice, simple girl that I am, nothing complicated you know, when suddenly he gives me this dirty look
and signals me to keep going up, up, up! He just couldn't wait
for me to get to the top. Okay, I say, okay, I'm going, then I say
in English, keep cool, man!
And I go up. I'm at the third rung.
Meanwhile, down on the ground, he's opening the box. The
box with the machine in it. Which I was impatient to get a look
at, only thing was I had to keep climbing. So I climbed.
But I'd barely gotten to the fourth rung when I said to myself
no, Georgette, there's no way, you can't go on like this, you'll
never get to the top if you don't come to a decision, the gold
lamé sheath is fine for hobbling around in but not for scaling
the heights of an umpire's chair... So, you really don't have that
many options, baby, in fact you have exactly one: get rid of that
dress once and for all.
Fine. I climb down the first four rungs, I unbutton my coat, I
take it off, I take off the dress, I put the coat back on. Just then,
I hear the loony yelling at me, real loud: What are you doing
down there? Dammit! We haven't got time to waste! Get back
up there! Come on, you haven't much time! Hurry up!
So, I obeyed. Like a servant. First rung, second rung, third rung,
fourth and fifth, finally, I notice that my temp work employer
had stopped watching me climb, and had gone back to his
machine...

There's your train. I'll have to talk to myself, now...
I don't mind.

'Cause at night I have the phosphorescent armbands of the rail-road switchmen to keep me company. I see them in the distance waving around, over there, near where track A crosses track B, and in the middle of all this darkness they look like fireflies.

Thanks for the cig.

Sixth rung, seventh rung... I look down. I see my gold lamé dress, in the late afternoon sun, looking like a snake's skin some snake left behind.

Eighth rung, ninth rung...

At the tenth rung, I realized that my hair was also getting to be too much for me. Those big piles of hair that I hadn't tried to manage for centuries, which were kinda like mattress stuffing, or uncarded wool... It was time to cut it off and I did.

Yes. I had a pair of scissors on me. I always remember to keep a pair of scissors on me. Right now, in fact, I have a pair on me.

My poor old hair... I saw it fall and then fly along the ground, that was something special in the region, that little wind blowing along the ground, the people around there say it's a bad wind, that it gives you the blues, terrible blues that stick to you and stay with you... It has a pretty name, though. But I've forgotten what it is.

I've forgotten a lot of things, since that incident with the Englishman.

Before he came along, I still had all my wits about me. And all my memory.

But memory is like a muscle. You can train it, exercise it, get it back again.

I start up again, fast as possible, from the tenth rung, determined to make up for lost time... But at the twelfth rung, my curiosity gets the better of me, and I say to myself Georgette, the lunatic must have calmed down by now, now's the time to check out the machine in the box...

It was some kind of automatic catapult mounted on what was probably an electronic brain, and on the other side of the catapult there was a little round opening, like a porthole, the whole thing in formica. A kind of formica. Light gray. With another round opening at the top of the machine, a wider hole where the Englishman was dropping his tennis balls, one by one, and inspecting them, one by one, in case they had any defects... There must have been more than a hundred... Only a crazy person would have that much patience.

I want to emphasize they were the old-fashioned kind of tennis balls. White. He must have been a snob, too, that Englishman, besides being loony.

I reached the thirteenth, the fourteenth, the fifteenth rung, and from time to time a flash of yellow would streak across the sky, it was my ring, my topaz, it wasn't going to be there long, but I didn't know that yet. Little by little, it got dark, I went on, I climbed higher without saving my strength... But by the twenty-eighth rung, I needed to catch my breath, I stopped.

And there far below me now, off in the countryside, were housetops and more housetops, rooftiles and more rooftiles, a country town spread out before my eyes, and it was me discovering these things, me who'd never seen anything before in my whole life as a stupid fool, and I said to myself, hell, Georgette, do you realize how lucky you are, look around you, applaud and respect what you see, those tiles, there are pink ones, there are red ones, there are orange-colored ones, and ocher, and dark ones, and light yellow ones, and all of them mixed with pale gray and eggshell white, china blue and verdigris, and all that just on one roof, and not one of those roofs looks like the one next to it, not one of the tops of any of those cypress trees looks like any other, and your gaze, this is what it is, it can go out, it can come back, it can flow, it can circle around, it slides quickly or it takes its time, and no matter how old you are you still can see well enough, yes you can, to find something new right in the middle of all these manmade roofs... And yet every one of those roofs was built just like its neighbor, 'cause as you know, men are just plain pig-headed and once they've perfected their little techniques, that's it, no more changes...

So there I was, by myself high above all those things, and suddenly I had a feeling. And what a feeling. It almost came bursting out of me, that's how good it was, I hadn't felt that way since I was young, those moments in the morning when all it takes is the tiniest little thing, you want to go out and kiss the world, you want to laugh and you want to cry when you see the morning you've been given, yes, I was up there perched on that rung of the ladder reliving that thing from my youth that I thought was dead and buried, oh, I'd have liked to dance, well, that is if I hadn't been perched up there on that dumb ladder... So, to make up for not dancing, I did something else instead, I took off my topaz ring and threw it up to the sky...

And it was as if the sky began to laugh...a beautiful, yellow laugh, all sparkly. And when the laughter disappeared, I saw a jet plane in front of me, far off in the distance, traveling straight across the horizon, its white line behind it, and then it vanished, too, but not the white line, its line broke up into white flakes just as the moon began to appear, a stupid, chalky moon which added another white to my collection: the white of the chair I was climbing toward, the long white trail behind the plane, the tennis clothes and the headband, all white, that the loony had on, the old-fashioned white tennis balls, some of my white hair which the wind hadn't yet blown away, a whisp of white fog wedged in between a church and two houses, the white smoke some squat little factory was spewing into the air through its chimney, two puffy white sores, creamy yellow inside, that grew on the face of the moon as I was making up my little inventory... And there were others, too, different whites, that I would never get to see, inasmuch as I had to put my foot on the twenty-ninth rung, then on the thirtieth, and the thirty-first...

And that's when it occurred to me that I would have to get rid of another piece of clothing as soon as possible, because now

I was really hot, my cheeks were burning, a sort of feverishness, I hadn't felt hot in so long, it took me a while to get used to the idea, the cold spell was over, and so there I was, but uh-oh, I was getting dehydrated now, and nothing on me to drink, and no way could I count on the Englishman... So I took off my coat and I tied it by the two sleeves to the thirty-third rung, thinking Inch'Allah, as the Arabs say, let's hope the wind doesn't get any stronger...

Finally. The Englishman had just finished programming his new equipment when I put my foot down on the thirty-sixth rung... And I could see farther off into the countryside... I saw fields of espaliers, I saw olive trees, I saw teeny-tiny people with drinks in their hands sitting in front of their houses, they made me thirsty, I would've liked to climb down then but I had to keep climbing, and I went on, climbing up and up... Thirty-seventh rung, thirty-eighth, thirty-ninth, and then, there I was.

I sat down.

It was no easy chair, that's for sure. But it was better than nothing.

I could relax.

I cast my eyes down at the court.

Not exactly a kindly look on the Englishman's face, at that point. Nope, a dirty one, meaning when you're ready, madam, we may commence.

I gave him the royal nod...

He stood in position, some distance from the machine...

Then it began: the balls came flying out at him, thrown from the machine, and there were two different ways they could be thrown: either as a backhand stroke or a forehand stroke. When it was a forehand stroke, the ball came down the barrel, stayed suspended in place as you'd expect, then flew out. Nothing fancy, just straight ahead. But when it was a backhand stroke, the ball would spin backward, a kind of back somersault at the muzzle of the barrel, then it would shoot out diagonally.

So we were just at the preliminaries. Round one of the warm-ups. Round one with the machine.

But he faced off against this machine exactly as if he had an enemy in front of him. He forgot that he was the one who'd programmed everything, forehand strokes, backhand strokes, and the amount of time between each ball. Because it wasn't always the same amount of time, necessarily. He would stand ready for a forehand stroke, the ball would come at him from the other side, and he'd run, the poor old thing, he'd run, his shoulder at ground level, and he'd sweat, and I'd see him all covered with strands of saliva and snot in the evening light, looking like a silk worm, some kind of insect busy spinning a cloak for himself...

And I was up there, calm as you please, in the cool air, all caught up in his game almost in spite of myself, good looking guy and what energy, really you had to admire him, I admired him so much that I forgot about the money I was going to earn... Until the moment when the machine spewed out its final ball. With what sounded like a dying man's last breath. Which brought me back to reality.

Around me it was night, by then. Real night, navy blue. We looked at each other, the lunatic and I. Then he bowed his head. With a nice smile. A sweet smile. He rubbed his neck. He looked like a guy with deep thoughts, a lifetime of thoughts. His hand was shaking. He'd aged ten years all of a sudden. I didn't want to see it, I told myself look somewhere else, Georgette, leave the poor crazy alone with whatever's in his head...

Elsewhere the world was the same. With its clumps of houses, high or low, crummy or high-class, but now from every window, that blue light from the TV sets turned on, throbbing like a vein, and above me millions of stars, and off to the left, the moon, having taken full advantage in the meantime, so big now it looked phoney, all reddish...

I look back down at the court, I see my Englishman walking around in circles. Finally he picks up a ball, and just like that, for no reason, serves the ball beautifully, right outside the court.

There's no sound of it bouncing, the ball gets lost in the shrubbery. And he starts to laugh, that weirdo. A deep, hearty laugh. Georgette, I say to myself, keep in mind, baby, that's what lurks beneath a charcoal-gray three-piece suit, simple yet elegant. Then he stopped laughing with a sharp little click of his jaws. And there was this silence. This long, oh so long silence. I fell asleep. That's when I fell asleep. I think.

Yes.
There are people who just can't stand silence.
I'm used to it. I've been here talking for so long without anybody answering me.
There are times too when I go without talking. They can be long, too.

I don't know how long I slept.
It's the last train. After you, there'll be nobody else. When I think. You're the only one and the train's going to stop just the same. Do you realize what that means, by any chance?
He doesn't really give a damn. In a hurry to catch his train. What's with all these people who are in such a hurry? Am I ever in such a hurry? And yet I should be. I have things to do, you know. Gotta get out of here. Gotta get my things together before I get out.

I don't know how long I stayed asleep. But I certainly know how he woke me up. I felt this wild shaking down in my lower back, it was coming from the chair, twisting my spine all around, I glanced down below, it was him all right, he was pounding like a madman on the lower rungs, Hey! Wake up! You're forgetting our contract! If you don't watch me you're not going to get a thing!
I assured him that I was wide awake and that I was all eyes, that he should watch out and not get overexcited, that a real champion should know how to manage his energy supply.

The word manage must have touched a nerve, how else do you explain what he shouted at me right then: You've seen me in action, well, I started out picking up tennis balls, see! When you come right down to it, they're really only toys!

Then he turned away from me, went to his gym bag and got out the whisky bottle, allowing himself two generous-sized gulps... He was making me thirsty, that bastard, and I was sure he knew it... But I had to watch him, that's what I was getting paid for. Which he didn't fail to remind me of before he went back to his game.

And here's what I saw, the second part of his match: He started by lowering the height of the net, after that he went over to the board next to the stands and made a few marks on it, he blew into his hands, and he fixed his headband, and then, for his crowning achievement, he began to play against himself. That's right, against himself.

Right off, I soon figured out that there was one position for him to serve from on one side of the net, and another, on the other side, for his opponent.

The basic thing was pretty simple: Firstly, he had to throw the balls as high as possible, and then go and return them from the other side of the net. Secondly, he had to change sides to serve when he was playing from the opponent's position. And he would serve from right at the net. Which took a certain adroitness, the serve had to be high but not too short.

I watched that and I said to myself, Georgette, this one's ready for the funny farm, all right, but you gotta hand it to him, show respect for any man who puts out that kind of effort.

I respected him but I laughed. And I hadn't laughed for so long...

Of course, what the whole thing meant was the time for the average game was short. Very short. Hardly time enough to say boo. And in spite of everything, he took time out, between each game, to go and mark down his scores on the board. And then he came back and started over again. Bloody elbows, bloody knees, injuries on both sides, on his own side as much as on the opponent's side, but he would yell out encouragement on each side of the net, just to be fair: Superb player on grass, a real specialist! Superb on grass and just as good on a hard court!... The man's whole egocentric nature was already coming to the fore that July, it was the beginning of a rivalry that would fascinate America for over a decade, over a decade, over a decade...

Now and then, he seemed to get stuck in a groove. Usually that was after a particularly heated exchange...

Get your elbow up, you jerk, get your elbow up!

I can't lose against such a bum, I can't!

Marvelous. That man was fighting against time, as well. And, on top of everything else, he had a bloody nose, which I've always found touching, in a man. And so, of course, at some point I applauded, I shouted bravo, bravo, with no thought to my own comfort, so as to make him understand that as unchallenged king on grass, packed dirt or synthetic courts he didn't need to prove himself to anybody... But the more I applauded the more he yelled, he was trying to drown me out, acting like a wild man: But if he keeps this up he's going to hit himself right between the eyes with his racket! He's going to put his own eye out, that dummy! Get your elbow up, way up! Come on! And loosen up the muscles in your calves, while you're at it! Come on, you've got it man, you've got it! If you don't shut up right this minute, I'm coming up there! I'm coming up there and I'll break you in two!

This last little endearment was addressed just to me.

So I shut up.

He wrote down his scores for the fourth game.

And on it went: the forehand drive, pull your racket back, you've got it man you've got it, the man's whole egocentric nature, etc. etc.

The blood got mixed in with the hair on his body, all reddish that hair, meanwhile he had dropped his shirt, he looked like some animal, cornered...

And it was right about the middle of the fifth game that I realized he was cheating.

And what was this cheating?

It was like this: More than once I saw him serve the ball, on purpose, NOT AS HIGH when he had to reach it from his position as the opponent than when he had to reach it from his own position...

So at the end of the fifth game, while he was writing down his scores, I stood up on my chair and shouted: Fault! Fault! Correct the scores! You weren't serving as high to the opponent as to yourself! Correct the scores!

He called me a few nasty names, but he made the corrections. I only saw him from the rear, while he was changing the scores. Amazing. He had suddenly aged. Gotten much smaller. He didn't even take up as much space as he had at the beginning. Finally, he launched into the sixth game.

And at that point I fell asleep, again.

Again he woke me up, this time to tell me the final results: You can applaud now. Now's the time! I've won! Do you hear! Won!

I go: You won the first set. You've got to play another one. Whatsa matter? Think I don't even know the basics?

He goes: What about the money? Your hundred francs? Aren't you in any hurry to collect your money?

I go: I'm tired. I lived up to my end of the bargain. Unlike you. After the first set, you're supposed to play another one.

He goes: And the flowers? Where are the flowers? Where are the flowers that they bring the winner?

And then I closed my eyes, and went back to sleep.

When I woke up, the day was already well underway. The sun

was right over my head.

At my feet, the court was empty. And all the balls were still there. Farther off was a small patch of grapevines on the side of a hill; above it a thrush and two of its mates were reeling through the air, like drunkards.

They reminded me how thirsty I was.

I started back down the rungs. Harder to climb down that chair than it was to climb up it.

I picked up my coat again on my way down.

I'm sticking with this coat. I'll stick with it right up to the end. 'Cause it was able to show me what it wanted. I was standing in my closet that morning looking for something to wear and all at once I saw it rise up from the shelf above and it pounced on me, it was squeezing me so hard I was suffocating, it got dark, it was like—

When I got down to the court I went up to see the score board a little better. He had erased all the scores. In their place he'd written four words that I couldn't read. Nobody could've read that writing, I tell ya. A retard's writing.

He'd put the hundred franc note right below the board, a stone to hold it in place. At least he kept his word.

And next to the money, his bottle of whisky. The same one as today. There was a little left in it, I drank it, and that's when I got a permanent taste for it.

I found my tote bag at the foot of the chair, no problem, but looking on the stands, no more suitcase. Somebody had decided he wanted it for himself. When you get right down to it, it was one less burden for me. Which meant that I got to the highway pretty fast once I left the dirt road.

You're a nice man. You're right, it's much nicer in this waiting room. But you'll get in trouble because of me. So I'm leaving.

You know it's against the rules to shut me up like this in the waiting room. Yes, I'm cold. But I'm well covered, ya know. So I'm leaving. One of these days. All you've got to do is change the glass covering over the picture, and I'll be out of your way. Meanwhile, thanks just the same. But wait a minute, your cap, don't you think that—

They leave you standing there in the middle of a sentence. No respect. Okay, so he's got more to do than just listen to me. They're waiting for him at home.
But there was a time when I had people waiting for me, too. 'Cause I've been waited for just as much as I've waited. Even-steven.

I'll leave when I feel like it.
Nothing's holding me here.
It's certainly not for any glass covering.
But if she'd just let me water her plants.
A cleaning woman who doesn't even want you to help her out, does that sound normal?
She spends ten extra minutes every morning watering her flower pots.
I tell her I'll be happy to do it for you, she doesn't even answer me. It's 'cause of my rags, they think I'm a nut. They don't realize that I'm cold.
Required routes for all employees assigned to travel to and from offices signal posts locomotive shops or switch yards. Those employees whose duties require travel between offices signal posts locomotive shops or—

I tell her I could water your flower pots for you, she doesn't even answer me.
The result is she goes on watering them in the morning because she's on the morning shift. And that's really not good for the flowers.

Especially not for those flowers, they can't take it. They're fragile flowers, delicate. All it takes is the tiniest little thing and they die.

That'll serve her right. Once they're dead, she'll have to replant them.

Only thing is, by the time they've grown again, Georgette won't be around to water them for her. Georgette will be long gone by then.

'Cause it's not for any glass covering, rest assured.

≈

Fatima Gallaire

Madame Bertin's Testimony

Translated from the French by
Jill Mac Dougall

UBU REPERTORY THEATER PUBLICATIONS
NEW YORK

Fatima Gallaire studied literature in her native Algeria following independence, at a time when few Algerian women were pursuing a college education. She continued studying in France where she obtained a degree in film studies. She has written poetry and short stories as well as twenty plays treating traditional North African themes and contemporary issues. Her work has been translated into English, German, Swedish, Russian, Uzbek, Spanish, and Hebrew. Her first play, *You Have Come Back (Ah! Vous êtes venus...là où il y a quelques tombes)*, translated by Jill Mac Dougall and directed by Françoise Kourilsky, was given its world premiere by Ubu Repertory Theater as part of the 1988 New York International Festival of the Arts and published in *Plays by Women: An International Anthology.* Treating the theme of religious intolerance, the play remains tragically pertinent today. *Madame Bertin's Testimony (Témoignage contre un homme stérile)* premiered in Metz in 1987 and was published concurrently by the French theatre journal *L'Avant Scène.* Fatima Gallaire has received two major awards honoring her work as a whole: the 1990 Prix Arletty and a 1994 award from the Académie française.

Jill Mac Dougall has been active in theatre research and production, in translating plays, and in teaching in Europe, Africa, and North America for over twenty years. In addition to her translations for Ubu, she has translated works for New Dramatists, the Centre d'essai des auteurs dramatiques in Montreal, *Women & Performance,* and *Canadian Theatre Review.* Her translations published in the Ubu Repertory Theater Publications series include *The Eye* (Zadi Zaourou), *The Girls from the 5 and 10* (Abla Farhoud), *Lost Voices* (Diur N'Tumb), *You Have Come Back* (Fatima Gallaire), *Burn River Burn* (Jean-Pol Fargeau), *The Crossroads* (Josué Kossi Efoui), *That Old Black Magic* (Koffi Kwahulé), *The Orphanage* (Reine Bartève), and *Game of Patience* (Abla Farhoud). Jill Mac Dougall holds an M.A. in Theatre Arts (University of Quebec at Montreal) and a Ph.D. in Performance Studies (NYU). She is currently teaching theatre and acting with Pennsylvania State University.

To April and Nassar Boukadoum,
my distant and dear cousins from Texas
who made me love America

TRANSLATOR'S NOTE

Mme. Bertin is one of the most fascinating characters I have ever translated. Full of the contradictions which make up poetry and human nature, her identity is as mysterious as the therapeutic ritual of her "testimony." I have attempted to preserve the character's inherent mystery while making the staging as concrete as possible. I thank Fatima Gallaire for her complete trust in my rendering of her words and leave further interpretation of Bertin's ambiguous testimony to other readers, directors, and actors.

JILL MAC DOUGALL

AUTHOR'S NOTE

When I was fifteen I dreamt of becoming a writer. In high school I wrote poems and kept a diary. I later destroyed everything, afraid my parents would discover my adolescent yearnings and marry me off as soon as possible.

After independence I began writing for Francophone journals. There were many of us then in Algiers, aspiring young writers emerging from seven years of boarding school and experimenting with freedom in the capital, far from parental supervision. We dabbled in university studies and earnestly reconstructed the world in the city's cafés.

The farmers scratched the land to feed us and we wrote for the country.

I, like many born of the Algerian bourgeoisie, felt the need to see if the grass was greener on the other side. Under the pretext of furthering my studies I headed straight to the arms of our former colonial mother, to France.

Having no financial aid or official status, I found work in a French nursing home. These retirement homes were more like living tombs representing every form of human misery steeped in loneliness. I diligently kept a journal, filling thirty notebooks, hoping perhaps to acquire the distance necessary to make a comedy from the tragedies of the "declining years" that I was witnessing.

In the uprooted solitude of my daily life those first years in France I found friendship, understanding, and complicity among the nursing home residents. I gave back the affection of a daughter or a granddaughter. I could not help but love these elderly people, who in my country would have been synonymous with goodness and wisdom, but here seemed rejected and forgotten.

They returned my affection and they confided in me. They lived in despair, but they were often incredibly lucid and affectionate. They were sometimes cynical, without hope for a world that had cast them off. They were never insane.

Insanity is a comforting label, a facile erasure of the violence of life which "normal" people evoke to reassure themselves. Mme. Bertin is not crazy. She talks to herself in order to relocate each event, to make sense of her life, to cleanse her mind and her soul.

This is a play about love and symbiosis in a couple, about the tender sensuality of the aging, about the violent sweetness of the end of life. Mme. Bertin's testimony is crude and cruel, disturbing as were our awakenings at twenty.

FATIMA GALLAIRE

SET

A double room in a nursing home. Morning. The room has not yet been cleaned. A bleached, yellowed screen hides a wash basin.

Two small night tables flank the white iron beds. Two metallic chairs stand in the corners, completing the institutional framing.

On a small table are two trays piled with remnants of breakfast. The decor is aseptic, cold. In the midst of this impersonal atmosphere are three surprising and magnificent pieces: a baroque dressing table with a high mirror, an armchair of mahogany and burgundy velvet, and a framed enlargement of a wedding picture.

CHARACTERS

MME. BERTIN, *A resident at the nursing home.*

The following characters, who interrupt Mme. Bertin's monologue, are minor; their only function is to shed greater light on Mme. Bertin's personality:

MARIE LAURE, *A nurse's aide.*

THE DOCTOR

ROSE, *Mme. Bertin's neighbor.*

CLAIRE, *An ergotherapist.*

THE WOMAN, *Mme. Bertin's double.*

What is commonly referred to as "an elderly woman" is seated in the armchair in front of the dressing table. She is giving the last touches to her hair and makeup. Her gestures are slow, deliberate, and elegant.

She stands and inspects herself in front of the mirror. She parades before the mirror, critical but proud. She examines her profile, tucking in her stomach and pulling her shoulders back to accentuate her bust, adjusting her bra or her girdle. She is wearing a long dress of light wool, a silk scarf and suede pumps. She is extremely well-groomed.

She is a seductive woman despite her age. Her movements are graceful. Her voice is deep and self-assured. Mme. Bertin has always resisted the bleakness of her surroundings.

After a final look in the mirror, she pushes the armchair to face the audience and to have a good view of the wedding portrait, which she will address periodically during her speech. She picks up a leather-bound wedding album and settles back into the armchair, murmuring to herself.

Noises from the outside drift into the room: wheel-chairs and nurses' carts, buzzers and telephones, feet scampering down the corridors, voices calling orders, muffled replies, grunts. After a moment lost in her reverie, Mme. Bertin fluffs her hair nervously and decides to reveal her testimony out loud to the audience.

Mme. BERTIN: *(throaty laugh)* To tell you the truth, I always thought this marriage business was idiotic. But after all, you can't expect a proof of love to be rational. Our families were so happy at the wedding, you should have seen them. And our friends, Lord were they happy...especially the girls. They were so afraid I'd reach thirty and become an old maid.

Not afraid for me as much as for themselves. I was perfectly happy single.

I was something of a black sheep in our group. In my neighborhood—I'm from the Thirteenth Arrondissement, pure Parisian roots you might say—I was a freak. Most of the girls I'd played with and gone to school with thought being happily single was a sign of social deviance. I didn't realize this right away. I kept going to see my friends who kept getting married and having children. I didn't have any kind of ardent desire to have a man in my bed. Some said I was cold, distant, perhaps frigid.

To this day I don't understand exactly what that means. I never had a father, so I guess I never felt the lack of a man. I pity those who jump on the first opportunity in search of the absent or abusive father.

No. I worked, I visited my mother, and I went to the movies. I was really a suspicious character when you come right down to it. I didn't need a man and I thought life was the greatest gift on earth.

Until one day I started noticing my friends were giving me strange looks. You know, a look counts a lot. You should always pay attention, even if it's bad, shocking, or judgmental. It's better to know how you're seen. Sometimes you are startled by a tender look, so sweet it melts your heart. Someone you thought very distant, but who has been saying good things about you behind your back... That's a delightful surprise, like the violent sweetness of honey.

But generally, alas, it is the opposite. Someone you thought a close friend, someone who seemed just like you, thinking you can't hear her, launches a scathing indictment. You can't even figure out why... What would have driven such and such a friend to be so resentful? Because you have blue eyes or black eyes? Because your hair is straight and hers curly, or the opposite? Or because you get along fine without a husband and she doesn't? Or because, for some absurd reason, she thinks you have your eye on her husband? Or worse, she thinks you can't live without your own husband and she hates you for being such a naturally happy couple. In my twilight years I have come to one rather disenchanting conclusion: life, apparently simple, is in fact very complicated.

(Gazing at the picture on the wall) Anyway, for some odd reason my marriage really delighted everyone. It's only now this appears obvious. It wasn't so clear to me then. When you're twenty-five, what do you know about life? Ridiculously little. So very, very little. So incomplete what you think you know.

My truth then was quite simple... I've always lived a modest life—I don't mean materially, my mother and I were better off than it appeared—I mean simple needs, uncomplicated. From the conventional wisdom my mother gave me I concluded that life was to be taken as it came and it was good. Yes, just that, a fine gift. I've never subscribed to the theory that pain is the meaning of life. It's not just a lesson I learned. It's in my very fibers, in my skin, in my natural spontaneity.

Everyone was happy the day of the wedding... It was in the middle of August...a plain civil ceremony, just a few of our friends glad to see us at last joining the ranks. A lazy day of fun with the promise of a wedding feast, a cake...

She flips through the pages of the wedding album, then comes to rest on a picture. Her hands linger on the page.

I even made the mayor cry. They told me this later. I was too busy wiping away my own tears. But it must be true if you look at the close up of the bride, the only one taken at this historic event. Historic because it would never happen again. There I am, trying to dry my tears and say yes at the same time.

> *Pause. Her gaze moves back to the enlargement on the wall. Among a friendly group the bride and groom smile back at her. They are touching in their shyness and rigidity.*

(Turning back to the audience) It's strange how year after year you can be moved by something so insignificant, something you've told yourself doesn't count at all. I was never fashionable... I've always been rather marginal. People who liked me said I was kind of odd. "Odd" in their mouths was a compliment. A compliment laced with envy. Have you noticed some people are incapable of being odd? With them any spark of fantasy, any hint of folly is seen as a sign of lunacy. It's sad.

Besides, my oddness had nothing aggressive about it. Even this marriage... I mean, no one could say "Ah-ha, you see...she's been craving sex and now she's making it legal."

Not really. Yet I was...how should I say...simply overflowing with a sort of spring fever.

I've never been what you might call pretty. *(She leans toward the audience.)* You see my face is rather plain. My looks leave much to be desired. But at twenty-five I was full of life and a twenty-five year old's desire to rush into life. My mother wanted to hold me back. She asked me why I was getting married. She wanted a dramatic explanation for why I was leaving her:

"You went to bed with him?" she asked.
"Lord, no."
"You must be pregnant."

"Mother!"

"Aren't you?"

"For heaven's sake, no."

"Then he dragged you off to the woods where he touched your heart and the softest spot on your body and now you can't live without him. Is that it?"

"Mother, I'm having a hard time following this conversation."

"I can see that. You don't seem to have any idea what I'm talking about. Just why are you getting married then?"

"Because he asked me to."

"I'm not interested in his reasons... It's obvious he's crawling at your feet, 'though God knows why. I don't want to upset you, but you know you're not exactly a prize catch."

"Mother, I don't know if your motive is to keep me here, but you've been telling me that long enough to get the idea."

"Just why are you marrying him anyway?" she insisted.

"Because I like him well enough. He's very nice. You can't say that about all men. They all seem to have something to prove. It's exhausting. He's...different."

It seems I was absolutely radiant after my marriage. Close friends told me I was brimming over with happiness. Others whispered with evil joy that I must have really been itching for it, because now that I had it I looked really good.

Everyone said it was a marriage made in heaven...a marriage of love. *(Dreamy, she pauses and massages her hands.)* I suppose it was. Yes, that's true. A marriage of love.

There's an Arabic proverb that says marriage is like a kettle of cold water you put on a low fire and wait until it boils. And if you wait long enough, it does; it boils and boils.

In this country we began "marrying for love" ages ago, in spite of our elders' reservations. So we put an already boiling pot on the fire. This created a few problems. Sometimes you get burned. Or you have to put out the fire...then it gets cold.

There was a certain balance to our relationship. I gathered he loved me but feared me. One day he told me it was because of my internal authority that he loved me and because he thought it might engulf him that he feared me. Really? I was astounded.

I loved him in a cautious way. I couldn't help it. I must have inherited a tacit mistrust from my mother which prevented my getting close to people. Thank God. I expect otherwise I would have been destroyed a long time ago.

(With an incredulous laugh) From this marriage which, according to our friends and enemies, was made in heaven, I was the only one who ever understood the truth. The underlying truth. The plain truth hit me on our wedding night. That blissful day, that very night...

(Silence. Then she bursts out.) He felt compelled to play the rooster. It all happened in the dark. It's not like today when you examine your partner from every possible angle before making any kind of decision. Poor Fernand...because, sorry to say, that is his name, some people are just doomed from the start to be ridiculous...he worked so hard. He mounted me two or three times, grunting and panting for a few seconds. These assaults were supposed to give me pleasure. Frankly, after all the toasts we'd imbibed during the wedding feast I hardly expected nor desired such a performance.

This is called "honoring your wife." The men who wrote the bible obviously never consulted any new brides. I was exhausted and all I wanted to do was sleep, sleep, sleep. We had a whole life together to prove our love for each other. This mounting and dismounting was more dishonorable than anything else. True, I didn't know much about sex, but he was so handsome and worldly I thought, a bit of a Don Juan in my eyes... "He must know all about these things," I thought. I was trapped.

Understand that I am a tolerant person, even a bit indulgent, a trait that probably comes from my origins as a bastard daughter. If you don't have a father around, you learn to keep your mouth shut. Whatever I might have been thinking, I remained very discreet.

Lord knows he performed his duty that night. Have you ever seen a rooster go after a hen? It's both ridiculous and fascinating. And just when you want to burst out laughing, the tragic aspect knots your throat. So the laugh or the cry won't escape, you tighten your mouth closed... I was going to say your ass. That too.

I said to myself: "Relax. If you relax, it won't hurt. Your girlfriends say it's wonderful. Malou says it's like going to heaven singing. Jeanine says you indeed feel honored one time out of two. Laure says, if you try, from time to time you understand what all the fuss is about. Just relax. There, there...relaxed, yes, like jelly."

There's my rooster with his thing out, looking for the entry point, bravely searching in the dark...

It's a game for a few moments, but it soon gets irritating. While Monsieur is looking for the entrance, he is weighing down on you with his 190 pounds of agitated muscle. Some pleasures are just not worth the effort it takes.

The only positive side to this tiresome nuptial initiation was that Fernand immediately lost any kind of husbandly prestige in my eyes. This would prove useful in avoiding errors and deceptions in the future. I knew what I was in for and did not entertain any foolish dreams...

Before he fell on me, I had visions of torture and rivers of blood. You can't imagine what horrors lurk in the minds of innocent virgins. But here I had gotten away with a mere sting from a small needle... Actually it's a rather pleasant memory.

My virginity was of the wider sort. Some are narrow, some flower shaped, some like stars or crescents. They say sometimes they're locked shut. Frequently there is no flow, a fact which men from those cultures where the hymen is so crucial are apparently unaware of.

At any rate, for me the experience was not physically painful. On the screen of my memory it does not appear as enlightening or traumatizing, but rather insignificant. The bride offers herself, it is her duty, her patriotic duty, equal those days to sacrificing yourself for your country...

Really? The truth is the woman opens her legs, the man climbs on top, humps her, then falls asleep. And he snores. You can't imagine how many snorers are being cursed by their spouses every night. And not just because they snore.

The poor man. I didn't despise him that first night. Hate is a slow process, the building of a life in common, brick upon brick. Hate demands daily nourishment. But right from the morning after I began seeing him with a cold, clinical eye. He never, never suspected the aberrational truth of his wife's sentiments.

Just look at him. *(She scrutinizes the picture.)* Such a trusting look, full of naiveté and complacency. It's rather touching.

She laughs to herself, as if remembering some dark but comical secret.

In all truth, I didn't hate Fernand for the nights in bed, but for the days. It's easy to see a man beating about under the sheets as ridiculous...especially from the icy and disillusioned standpoint of a woman who has never been hot. I was convinced that one night my Fernand would perform as we both expected and we would both be transported.

No, the problem was not the dark nights, but the harsh light of day. Here man has all rights and the woman performs her duty with gratitude.

(With an audible expression of disgust) What a crock of shit.

To live together means to breathe together, gasp at beautiful things together, play together, cry together, move together on the road of life with its ups and downs. I soon abandoned the idea that we would. Fernand breathed all by himself and my breath was worth nothing except to save him in dire circumstances. In everyday life he had little use for me. He didn't give a damn.

(Shouting, enraged) He didn't give a damn.

There is a timid knock at the door.

MME. BERTIN: *(obviously irritated by the interruption)* What do you want?

MARIE-LAURE: *(from behind the door)* Madame Bertin, it's Marie-Laure. Can I come in? I have to clean the room.

MME. BERTIN: If you must, *(under her breath)* idiot child.

The nurse's aide, a country girl around eighteen, enters. She is obviously terrified of Mme. Bertin and would prefer to get the cleaning done as fast as possible. She nods to Mme. Bertin before scampering to the breakfast trays.

MARIE-LAURE: So we ate almost all our breakfast today?

MME. BERTIN: WE did nothing of the sort. Would WE just move out and leave ME in peace? *(Marie-Laure stares at her blankly.)* Pick up and get out.

MARIE-LAURE: Mme. Bertin is in a bad mood today. M. Bertin has an appointment with the psychologist so I guess Mme. Bertin feels kind of alone, hunh? Is that it?

MME. BERTIN: Fuck off, little slut.

MARIE-LAURE: Mme. Bertin! Fortunately, nobody can hear you.

MME. BERTIN: Nobody? You hardly count, do you?

MARIE-LAURE: *(ignoring her last remark, going to make the beds and continuing to speak in the same determined, cheerful tone)* So we didn't make our beds this morning? Are we getting lazy?

MME. BERTIN: What the...? Are you bent on ruining my day?

MARIE-LAURE: *(finishing the beds, fluffing the pillows)* If I had thought twice, I would have waited till lunch to tidy up.

MME. BERTIN: Just shove off, little jerk. Can't you see I'm trying to think?

MARIE-LAURE: *(scuttling over to the screen which she pulls away to clean the wash basin)* Fortunately all our little grandmothers are not like you, otherwise I...

MME. BERTIN: You'd be out a job, wouldn't you?

MARIE-LAURE: They're very sweet, you know.

MME. BERTIN: Are you paid to henpeck me? I realize you're not paid very much, so I wonder if you don't enjoy harassing me? Do you know how much you annoy me?

> *After scouring the sink in silence, Marie-Laure puts the sponge on the shelf and replaces the screen.*

MARIE-LAURE: Mme. Bertin, I have nothing against you. Maybe I like you more than the others who treat me like a baby... If I chide you about the room it's because the ergo-what's-a-name...

MME. BERTIN: The ergotherapist?

MARIE-LAURE: Yeah. She says it's best you stay busy, otherwise you'll feel useless. It's good for you. All of you who can still walk about should make their beds.

MME. BERTIN: Never got laid properly.

MARIE-LAURE: Pardon?

MME. BERTIN: I don't mean you. I mean her.

MARIE-LAURE: Well, I like you anyway. If I wasn't so busy, I'd come to see you more often.

MME. BERTIN: *(speaking rapidly)* Busy, busy, busy... Keep them busy, wallowing in stupidity.

MARIE-LAURE: People say I'm not too smart. I was a foster child. I have trouble following you when you talk so fast.

MME. BERTIN: *(after a pause, gently)* Marie-Laure...

MARIE-LAURE: Madame?

MME. BERTIN: Do you have a sweetheart? A lover? A fiancé? A husband? A companion?

MARIE-LAURE: You mean am I with a man?

MME. BERTIN: That's it. A man.

MARIE-LAURE: Sure. We've been together for two years now.

MME. BERTIN: What does he like?

MARIE-LAURE: *(counting on her fingers)* Pancakes, spaghetti, fish cakes, and beef stew. But I'm not too good at the stew...

MME. BERTIN: Poor child...

MARIE-LAURE: You have to buy the beef, soak it all night in wine, clean all the vegetables... With this job, I don't have time. How can I think of all that ahead of time?

MME. BERTIN: You can't.

MARIE-LAURE: That's what I tell him.

MME. BERTIN: But that isn't what I asked.

MARIE-LAURE: It isn't?

MME. BERTIN: I asked you what does he like. In bed.

MARIE-LAURE: Oh. *(Pause.)* Nobody's ever...

MME. BERTIN: Are you going to answer instead of pretending to think about it?

MARIE-LAURE: Nobody ever asked such a thing.

MME. BERTIN: Well, I did. What does he like you to do for him?

MARIE-LAURE: I don't know if...

MME. BERTIN: What?

MARIE-LAURE: ...if I should say...

MME. BERTIN: That?

MARIE-LAURE: He likes me to...

MME. BERTIN: To?

MARIE-LAURE: To suck him.

MME. BERTIN: *(slapping her hands on her lap)* I knew it! They're all the same...pigs.

MARIE-LAURE: Pardon? Oh, Madame, have I shocked you? I shouldn't have said anything, please don't tell the director.

MME. BERTIN: I understand. He'd fire you.

MARIE-LAURE: Heavens no.

MME. BERTIN: *(very surprised)* Really? Then why?

MARIE-LAURE: The director wants me to do it to him.

MME. BERTIN: And you don't want to, is that it?

MARIE-LAURE: Yuck, no. Sometimes when I bring in his coffee he takes me from behind and that's about all I can stand. I've seen his dinky little white thing and I have absolutely no desire to kiss it. But Paul...

MME. BERTIN: Paul? Go on.

MARIE-LAURE: My Paul. At night when I see his big cock come up, so dark, so proud, it's so beautiful I want to eat it.

MME. BERTIN: I can imagine... And what does he do for you?

MARIE-LAURE: Pardon?

MME. BERTIN: Does he want to eat you?

MARIE-LAURE: Uh, yeah. How did you guess?

MME. BERTIN: I have some experience.

MARIE-LAURE: He loves to suck my boobs.

MME. BERTIN: Just your breasts?

MARIE-LAURE: What else?

MME. BERTIN: *(impatient)* Are you really so dense? What about your belly, down there, your lovely flower of flesh?

MARIE-LAURE: *(hesitating)* You mean...my pussy?

MME. BERTIN: Yes, that's what I mean.

MARIE-LAURE: Oh, no, Mme. Bertin. Nobody does that.

MME. BERTIN: Really? Who told you so?

MARIE-LAURE: He did. Paul. My man.

MME. BERTIN: Ah yes, the big man...

MARIE-LAURE: Yeah, but he's like a baby. He loves to be cuddled.

MME. BERTIN: And cuckold.

MARIE-LAURE: Oh, please don't tell anybody. If that gets around, the director will fire me for sure.

MME. BERTIN: *(softly)* No, I won't say a word.

MARIE-LAURE: Thank you, Mme. Bertin. I always thought you were better than the others. I mean you scare me, you're so gruff, but underneath I can tell you respect people. And you know a lot about life.

MME. BERTIN: Yes, yes. Move along now. You've wasted enough of my time.

MARIE-LAURE: *(picking up the breakfast trays and moving toward the door)* And remember, for your own good, you have the right to make your bed.

MME. BERTIN: *(snarling at her)* And my ass? Do I have the right to show my useless old ass?

MARIE-LAURE: *(frightened she might do just that)* Oh, no, please. Now I've gone and made you angry again.

MME. BERTIN: Never mind me. I'm just in a bad mood... You're a good kid. Remind me when it's your birthday. I'll try to be nicer to you.

MARIE-LAURE: Thank you, Mme. Bertin. I always knew...

MME. BERTIN: Would you just get out of here?

> *Marie-Laure exits. Pause. Mme. Bertin turns her attention back to her album.*

MME. BERTIN: *(nodding her head)* What an event! We had become husband and wife. To prove it he fulfilled his duty every night, pounding on me regularly, then falling off to sleep satisfied. But...no, that wasn't so bad. It was the mornings. You see I am very sensitive in the morning. I need time. Whereas he would charge into the day like a bull. His eyes half-closed and his breath reeking, he would attack at sunrise. In the movies you see these couples waking in the morning: lacy nightgown and silk pajamas, their hair skillfully disheveled, they move in for the first kiss of the day in close up.

(Shuddering) Blach. It's enough to make you vomit. Everybody smells disgusting in the morning. Especially the smokers. The secretions of the night are oozing from every pore and the most logical thing to do is go wash up. It's amazing that great civilizations blithely ignore this fact.

I finally got around to asking Fernand for an explanation of his daily morning blitz which never failed to take me by surprise. He had a ready answer. It seems he would wake in a state of arousal and, if he acted immediately, he could preserve his dream fantasies and avoid the feeling of guilt that often accompanies these activities. This was all news to me. I admit I had no idea it was so complicated. You never know what depraved thoughts lurk in a man's mind.

Fortunately for him, for us, I was young and healthy and lacked much imagination. At night, in the secret of our clumsy gropings, I would occasionally rise to heaven with him. But it was always so unexpected and, on his part, so accidental that I found it hilarious. This worried him.

"What's wrong? Why are you laughing?"
"Just because I feel good."
"You do? Well, that's fine, that's great."

He was as easy to reassure as he was to fool. I could have cheated on him without his ever suspecting a thing. But I wasn't interested. Basically I was fond of him and, even given the choice, I would not have exchanged him for a Prince Charming. What would I have gained? I realized early on observing other couples that Fernand in his naiveté was no worse than any man.

Pause. She brushes a thought aside before continuing.

As men tend to be, he was self-centered and very proud. This, coupled with his antics in our intimate moments, made him a ludicrous character. But I was the only one who could notice. I'm sure if the wives of great men revealed what they know, we'd be astounded by the pettiness, weakness, and bizarre tastes of these heroes.

As for Fernand I learned to tolerate and even occasionally to enjoy his nightly visits. I found my own pleasure, more or less. I began to participate, panting, even moaning. He, as always, would finish with a groan, roll over, and immediately begin to snore. I guess I said that already. Am I rambling?

(After a pause of deep thought) It wasn't the nights... Now I know I'm repeating myself, but I have the right to at my age. No, it wasn't the nights but the mornings that were dreadful. Sometimes I dreamt of killing him. It might have happened one morning. I dreamt of strangling him before he woke, just to have one day alone, without hearing him or seeing him or being near him. I felt that one day would be worth a life in prison. I could hardly have explained what I'd done to the police.

"Why did you kill him?" they would ask.
"For nothing."

Truly for nothing. As I said, he's no worse than another. For nothing... Or perhaps because of his whistling. He was a whistler, a harmless enough habit you'd say. I agree. Yet when you're cutting the potatoes for the soup or washing the lettuce this whistle becomes...it became unbearable. I don't suppose there was anything extraordinary about the whistle itself, but for me it was a physical aggression. It was like a voice someplace out there saying "You poor fool. Still slaving away while I'm enjoying myself. I read the paper, I smoke my pipe, I can even take a stroll if I wish. Poor idiot who has nothing better to do in life than cut potatoes, who thinks a nice tossed salad is the most important thing on earth. Damned right, lucky for me you do. By the way, I hope you didn't forget to pick up my tobacco for the weekend."

Oh, that whistle told me many, many things. I hated it more than anything else, even more than his creeping up behind me and grabbing my breasts while I was doing the dishes. Fernand adored my bosoms. Nature has well endowed me. I've always had a big bust, enviable I guess. Anyway it drove Fernand insane. The few times he was being creative making love, he would say feverishly "Climb on top of me and smother me with your bosoms. Come on. Hurry, smother me."

Since he had never managed to find my clitoris in all his groping, I didn't mind this arrangement. I would climb on him and, since they were quite plump when I was younger, my breasts would fill his whole face and eager mouth. And I could tickle myself by rubbing against him. I preferred this to his fumbling around in my vulva. His heavy hands pressing on me smashed any kind of desire. He didn't do this very often. I think he was afraid. I think he did try to find my sensitive point once or twice, and it's all to his credit, because men were not expected to do that in those days. But I have to tell you, in over fifty years of wedlock, he never, never managed to find the little bud of my flower.

A long pause.

True, it was partially my fault. As a wife, I behaved as passively as I had when I was a virgin. I let him do his thing on my body and never really intervened. The day was already exhausting and I had little energy left at night to satisfy both of us. Perhaps he should have married a more ardent and experienced woman. I don't know. He never complained.

A tacit agreement was established between us. One time he'd be on top and the next I would. It was quite friendly and arranged both parties. Lord, for the times, it was downright revolutionary. I could never have told my girlfriends about this. They would have taken me for a whore, a bitch in heat, daring to mount her husband for her own pleasure.

I doubt he ever told his friends either.

You know, I dreamt of killing him, yet I loved him. In some ways I loved him very much. I never revealed his weakness, never told anyone how he behaved in our private moments. Nobody spoke about those things then anyway. We just lived through them. I think it was wrong to hide everything. Because silence allowed for the worst kind of abuse. Against women of course. Women and sometimes children. I was never fortunate enough to be a mother and I have always wondered how women could accept that fathers and stepfathers touch their children. In that way I mean. I understand they were thinking of their own survival, but I can't imagine surviving on the back of my child. I could have dealt with any kind of abuse on myself. But if Fernand had ever dared touch one of our children, I would have killed him immediately. Before it happened. I would have seen it in his eyes well before he even made a move. And I would have found a way to be acquitted and come back to take care of my kids.

At any rate, the problem never presented itself. We never had children.

Pause.

I didn't really mind this. I was such a mother to my husband anyway. I always assumed our barren marriage as my responsibility, even after I went to see a specialist, a gyno-what's-a-name, a female malady doctor. You know, where you spread your legs like a dissected frog. I was brave enough to go on my own. No one had advised or even hinted I should do this. I just wanted to know the truth for my own sake. I learned that I was in fact perfectly capable of having broods of children. Therefore I was not the sterile one.

I decided... Was it out of respect for our friendship? Love? Out of a sense of sacrifice ingrained in women, a capacity to assume the immense silent pain? Why exactly? I suppose for all these reasons: friendship, love, sacrifice. Because I must have loved my poor husband. I decided never to tell him and to entertain the illusion that our lack of descendants was my fault.

Men are so sensitive. I believe if he knew the truth it would have broken him. He was, after all, a part of my daily life, and despite my occasional feelings of disgust, I had no desire to see him brutally driven to madness or suicide.

Damned fool... He didn't know how lucky he was to have found me. An ordinary woman with such plain looks and so little imagination. More than any other could, I protected him, cared for him, pampered him... *(She sobs softly.)*

> *She rises from her chair and goes to the dressing table. Languishingly, she moves back and forth in front of the mirror to a vague lullaby she hums under her breath. Her hands slide over her body, slowly caressing her breasts, her buttocks, her belly.*

Poor darling, for his times he was as good as they come. And I suppose that, under my complacent cow manner, I was a radical. I was not interested in survival at any cost, suffering for rewards in the hereafter and all that nonsense. What I wanted was pleasure, the joie de vivre. It's so simple. It seems people die without ever realizing this simple truth. *(A chuckle.)* A ripe cheese, a full-bodied wine, a little roll in bed when you're in the mood...nothing beats that. I didn't ever need a lesson to know nothing beats that.

> *There is a brutal knock at the door. A voice outside barks: "Bertin, go to the psychologist's."*

Startled, then inhaling deeply, Mme. Bertin barks back.

And you, go to hell!

A moment passes while she regains her composure. She returns her attention to the mirror which calms her. She continues caressing her body during the following speech.

I'm actually grateful to my husband, not for the pleasure he gave me in bed which didn't amount to much, but because of...because of the pleasure he excited me to seek in my own body. You see, marriage awakened my senses. Handled, however badly, my body was aroused.

I got in the habit of getting up at dawn to avoid my husband's early morning antics, his blitz assaults under the pretext his conscience was still asleep and he could get his jollies off by treating me as his wet nurse.

I became a morning person. This shift was not so difficult for a girl who was allowed to stay in bed or do whatever she pleased by an indulgent single mother. I learned to love seeing day break, being there to watch and honor the sun rising. Now, if you ask me to meet you at dawn in some train station, whatever the season, I'll be there.

I learned to appreciate those quiet moments when I could savor my coffee all alone and plan what I would do with my day. These solitary moments, pure, free of fatigue or distractions, were precious. Fernand, stuck alone in bed and fondling himself before his eyes opened, vaguely resented this time I had stolen from him.

She laughs softly while continuing to shape her body with light, spider-like gestures, as if to remind herself of its existence rather than to obtain sensual pleasure.

I didn't need to touch myself to feel an irrepressible joy rise straight up my spine. I assure you, I wasn't feverishly looking for sensations. Nor was it my simple enjoyment of life. It came at the most unexpected moments. I might be doing my housework, dusting or whatever, and all of a sudden an inexplicable desire would surge up. This delicious shiver I had in no way solicited would sometimes force me to collapse in the nearest chair.

> *She returns to the armchair and collapses, apparently spent. Her head lowered, her shoulders stooped, she sits a moment in silence.*

I needed these moments of solitary pleasure because...my poor Fernand...had become increasingly bizarre. I could no longer count on him for earthly joys. Oddly, the more his mind degenerated, the more attached I became. I passed from a short-lived period as a lover...yes, you would have to call it that, his lover...to the role of his mother. We entered the era of secret indulgences. You see, I...

> *A loud knock at the door.*

MME. BERTIN: *(furious)* What do you want now?

DOCTOR: *(behind the door)* It's the doctor. Time for your checkup.

MME. BERTIN: No kidding.

DOCTOR: Can I come in? Are you decent?

MME. BERTIN: *(snickering)* Decent...what could shock you anyway? Yes, come in, *(under her breath)* you quack in skirts.

The door opens and a young woman in a white coat enters. She wears the institutional smile and walks with the competent step of her rank. Mme. Bertin appears on the defensive.

DOCTOR: *(mechanically)* How is everything?

MME. BERTIN: To think I pay to have you around.

DOCTOR: Well, according to your file you don't pay that much. Do you?

MME. BERTIN: My husband never bought additional insurance. Are you here to scold me?

DOCTOR: Not at all. I just need to take your blood pressure. Do you mind?

MME. BERTIN: You'll do it whether I mind or not. Suppose I said yes, I do mind?

DOCTOR: Then I'd just leave and come back later. *(Business-like)* Roll up your sleeve now.

MME. BERTIN: *(grumbling)* Alright. Here.

Mme. Bertin rolls up her sleeve. The doctor takes her blood pressure.

DOCTOR: *(surprised)* You're way up there. What happened? Your blood pressure is usually low. Did something upset you this morning?

MME. BERTIN: Yes. Just seeing you upset me so much I thought

I'd throw a little bile your way.

DOCTOR: *(arranging her equipment)* You don't seem to be yourself today.

MME. BERTIN: You have no idea, pea brain.

DOCTOR: *(ignoring her remark)* So I'll come back later.

MME. BERTIN: *(growling under her breath)* Don't bother.

DOCTOR: Your voice is strange. It sounds like you have a strep throat. *(Ever efficient)* Let me take a look.

MME. BERTIN: *(violently)* Would you just fuck off?

DOCTOR: *(backing away, almost fearful)* I swear, some days I don't recognize you.

MME. BERTIN: I like to surprise people.

DOCTOR: Are you sure you're all right?

MME. BERTIN: I will be if you just move on. Leave me some space. Get out.

DOCTOR: Well, I know one thing. You have a strep throat.

MME. BERTIN: So are you going to call a press conference?

DOCTOR: I have other patients to see. I'll come back later.

The doctor exits at a hurried pace, slamming the door behind her.

MME. BERTIN: Good riddance, bitch, quack. *(She glances at her-*

self in the mirror and nervously puffs up her hair.) I need to go to the hairdresser's. My husband, Monsieur Bertin, seems to be spending a long time at the hairdresser's. People might begin wondering where he is.

She leans back in her armchair with a sigh.

Poor darling Fernand. He became rather strange as time went on. Some nights he would say to me "Turn around. I want to feel your sweet little ass against my belly. Put your cheeks around my sex. Do you feel it getting hard between your legs?" I did not hesitate. I wrapped my legs around his penis, but I remained on my guard. "Fernand, what do you want back there?" I asked. "To make love like dogs do. It's so good." He said something like that anyway. I don't remember exactly what.

Like dogs do. To come up with such fantasies shows you have no more pressing problems on your mind. Like the price of bread. I did not, after all, work for gainful employment. I just calculated how much money we needed to get food on the table. And the rent paid and not go into debt and hold our head high. Protected from these gnawing worries, he could relax. He could say "Take me in your cheeks" and I would comply. I lay in the fetal position, but I held my bottom shut, in case he mistook his route. Sometimes I fell asleep before he came. I didn't hear his groans. Nor his snoring. Thus I kept our friendship alive.

Divorce was not common in those days outside of dire circumstances. I understood a man's assuming women would always satisfy his whims because he had been brought up that way by mothers and aunts and grandmothers. One day he's grown up with a woman of his own. A wife, a toy, an object that doesn't talk back. So he goes on.

(Stifling a scream) So he goes on!

Silence.

Damn it, how could I hate him? Old as he is today, he's my sweetheart, my very dearest friend. A crazy old man. Crazy enough to go to a psychologist and spill out his problems. He comes back radiant. He gives me his arm and we go have a drink together before dinner. He claims he never really says anything, but how would I know?

I don't think I've judged him too harshly. I inherited a lot of tolerance from my mother. She was a saint. She carried her solitude like a cross. She worked like a slave. She taught me to bear up under suffering. As for human frailty, I've known more than my share and guessed the rest. Very young, I was already old. I saw through people like glass. I saw their perverse underside clearly. Practiced composure allowed me to remain calm while persons of supposedly irreproachable reputation endlessly proclaimed their virtues. I saw straight through to the backstage of their being and I didn't bat an eye... I suppose my bastard status made me tolerant and old before my time. Older than eternity. I had absorbed all the vices of the world, to understand them, to defend myself against them. No lie could surprise me anymore.

Then Fernand entered my life. On tip toe, taking me by surprise. He had beautiful eyes... I'm very sensitive to a look... Magnificent eyes. He looked at me tenderly one day in April and my heart melted.

Damn fool. With his cock-eyed balls. I didn't realize this till later, but Fernand has three testicles. One day I must find the courage to ask a doctor, one less quack than the others, about this anomaly. It couldn't be a serious problem since Fernand didn't die from it. He never even mentioned it. I've heard it has something to do with varicose veins. Odd, isn't it? Three lovely little nuts. Actually it's rather touching. For a woman in love, it's endearing. Oh, my baby has a sore-sore. Let Mommy kiss it and make it better, let Mommy lick it. And I did. You did. We did. People do. No sense in sticking your head in the ground. I have nothing to hide at any rate.

As the years went on Fernand became more and more charming, more debonair in public. No one suspected what he turned into when we were alone. He became more and more demanding in private. As I said, I was rather passive and let myself be manipulated as he pleased. I was a girl of my times and accepted everything as my wifely duty. He would say "Your thighs, your lovely thighs" and I would take him between my legs. "Your ass, your lovely ass" and I would curl up, tightening my muscles to protect what I could. "Your tits, your lovely tits" and I would hop on him so he could suckle and imagine he was having his wet nurse. No harm in all that.

Sometimes he begged me to touch him. In the dark I would bravely grab whatever he presented to me, trying to figure it all out. Sometimes it made me nauseous, sometimes it delighted me. In the dark, under the sheets...I did learn there were three, although I never saw them.

"Touch me there, there... Feel how big it is... You want it, don't you? I'll give it to you... Ah, ahh, there, I'm coming, ah, ayh-haa," until he finished in a yelp.

I remained calm in the middle of this storm, but I told myself that one day I would complain to the mayor. Remember all that baloney about "love, honor, and protect?" It was pretty one-sided, if you ask me. Marriage is not the happily-ever-after business it's cracked up to be, at least not for women. It's an institution invented by men for their personal comfort. If men thought they'd be better served by a sow, they'd marry a sow.

Pause. A knock at the door.

MME. BERTIN: Who is it?

ROSE: *(behind the door)* It's Rose.

MME. BERTIN: Come in, *(gnashing her teeth)* dear.

Rose, the neighbor, enters. She is dressed, but her hair is uncombed.

ROSE: *(peering around the room)* I thought I saw you go out earlier.

MME. BERTIN: Nope.

ROSE: Weren't we supposed to go to the hairdresser's together?

MME. BERTIN: *(sighing)* Yes.

ROSE: Then let's go.

MME. BERTIN: I don't feel like it.

ROSE: Don't you want to go to the birthday party this afternoon?

MME. BERTIN: You know I hate that silly crap.

ROSE: Gracious me. I see you're having one of your bad days.

MME. BERTIN: Right.

ROSE: Has Monsieur Bertin been mean to you this morning?

MME. BERTIN: *(hurt)* What are you talking about?

ROSE: Well, I've been a widow for years, but I know women suffer the most in a couple.

MME. BERTIN: Let me tell you something, Rose. You don't know a god damn thing.

ROSE: *(backing out)* Gracious. I guess I'd better leave you be... Anyway I have an appointment.

MME. BERTIN: Hurry up then. You don't want to be late.

Rose closes the door behind her.

MME. BERTIN: *(muttering)* Frustrated old fool. Busy body. Snake in curlers. Now she'll tell everyone at the hairdresser's what a foul mood I was in. Toothless blabber mouth.

A peremptory knock at the door.

MME. BERTIN: Oh for God's sake. What is it now?

A voice answers: "Bertin, go to the psychologist's immediately."

MME. BERTIN: He isn't here. He went to the hairdresser's.

She listens to the footsteps stalk off.

MME. BERTIN: *(suddenly weary, massaging her temples)* Why is everyone in such a hurry this morning? *(Laughing to herself)* I must be getting old. I could be a grandmother like Rose, even though I never had children. I doubt all those respectable and doddering old fools know what's on my mind. If they suspected how much I loved to fondle Fernand's divine fruit, they'd probably lock me up for good.

(Dreamy) Like plump grapes ripening on the vine. Delicious... Oh, not the way he imposed it on me, grunting "Go on, eat me, quick." No, I just wanted to play with them. Take them delicately in my fingers... I liked to stroke his penis when it was soft, whispering to it and moving ever so slowly so that the monster wouldn't rise up too quickly, hideously swollen and drooling. I just wanted to take my time. That's all I've ever wanted. Take the time to take the time. The time for poetry, for dreams, for play. I've always been very playful.

But he was always in a hurry. And so demanding. Any hour of the day. It was exhausting. Not only did he start early in the morning...and, excuse me, you might as well make love with a herd of goats at that hour...but he was obsessed the whole day through. He'd come home for lunch and stick his hand up my dress. It's not easy to turn an omelette in those conditions, believe me. He'd be at it again after dinner while I was trying to get the dishes done, and I've always despised washing dishes anyway. He told me he'd often dreamt of sleeping with the maid and that my little apron excited him. Can you imagine?

Gradually I became disgusted with his incessant needs. I thought "Too bad. We had some good times together." I considered going back to live with my mother. I simply couldn't stand to be around him anymore, couldn't bear the sound of his voice and that horrible whistle, couldn't stomach his stench of tobacco and animal in rut.

Then I reasoned with myself. Divorce was not the easy affair it is today. I had no grounds whatsoever, at least not in the eyes of the law or of our friends. He was a good provider and full of consideration for me, at least in public. Everyone thought he was a real gentleman. We were known as a happy couple. Inseparable.

Besides, I felt somewhat responsible for his obsessive behaviour. I figured if I stayed with him, I could limit the damage. Like a mother with a naughty boy. Yes, he was my little boy. *(Trembling with emotion)* Oh, my God.

> *She breaks out in tears. She fumbles for a handkerchief and wipes her cheeks before continuing.*

I got really terrified when I noticed him looking at our friends' children in a very specific and embarrassing way. No one else seemed to notice, thank God.

> *She blows her nose and tucks her handkerchief in her pocket.*

I probably perceived this tendency even before he did. So I took some precautions. To love someone else's children is a truly beautiful thing. When you have none of your own and you're suddenly struck by your own mortality, it is magnificent. You can go to your grave painlessly, singing even. But it's easy to slip into more dangerous territory. Children are not playthings. No.

Fernand never wanted to adopt a child. I suppose women are better prepared for this since they're used to sacrificing for others. This is their upbringing. A man raising someone else's child is more dangerous. You never know what might run through his mind.

(With a deep sigh) I feel oppressed. All these memories from such a troubled past, a past which appeared so blissfully ordi-

nary. We still seem ordinary. *(With a laugh)* We're still the perfect couple in everyone's eyes. Life is funny.

A knock at the door.

MME. BERTIN: What is it now? I'm plain worn out insulting people.

CLAIRE: *(behind the door)* Mme. Bertin? It's Claire.

MME. BERTIN: Come in, ergo-what'ch-ma-call-it.

> *An attractive woman in her early thirties enters. She greets Mme. Bertin with genuine affection.*

CLAIRE: Ergotherapist, as you know very well. But just call me Claire. How are you today?

MME. BERTIN: What's gotten into you? You look really perky.

CLAIRE: I just heard we've got funding for the crafts workshop. We're going to have a lot of fun together.

MME. BERTIN: What the hell do I care?

CLAIRE: But Mme. Bertin, you love crafts. And you're so gifted.

MME. BERTIN: So you're going to exploit me? Force me to crochet doilies and bedspreads one after another that you'll sell at your stupid craft shows while I nurse my arthritic fingers and don't get a blessed cent? Not for me, thank you very much.

> *Surprised by such a vehement statement, Claire approaches, leans down and looks closely at Mme. Bertin.*

CLAIRE: *(rising, with a falsely threatening tone)* So you're up to your old tricks, are you Mme. Bertin? Entertaining your little vices behind closed doors.

MME. BERTIN: And if you tell anyone, I'll wring your little neck. Oh, just drop it. I've run out of insults for you. You...worthless trash...you... You're a bastard child too, aren't you? Actually, I like you very much. I would have been happy to have a daughter like you. You see people clearly and that's a great quality. It shows you care enough to take a good look in a world dying of indifference.

CLAIRE: Mme. Bertin...

MME. BERTIN: Yes, my child.

CLAIRE: Why do you do that? Why do you torture yourself? Are you really so unhappy?

MME. BERTIN: No, not really. Torture is a form of therapy. Just between us, it's a kind of cure for me.

CLAIRE: *(sadly)* I suppose so. Maybe it's the new moon that gets you so riled up.

MME. BERTIN: And all those dim-wit charlatans, the so-called specialists snooping around...

CLAIRE: It must be exhausting for you.

MME. BERTIN: It is, I confess.

Pause.

CLAIRE: For the workshop, it's okay, come whenever you feel

like it. Just to lend a little atmosphere. You don't have to work. Just throw a few of your insults and four-letter words around to wake up the grannies. They seem shocked, but they love it.

MME. BERTIN: Well, if you put it that way... How can I resist?

CLAIRE: I've got to run now. See you later.

MME. BERTIN: Yes, run along. Get out of here.

> *Claire exits.*

> *Alone again, Mme. Bertin sighs and slumps in her chair. She has lost much of her imposing presence.*

> *A long moment goes by. Then the door opens and a woman rushes in. Coiffed and dressed exactly like her, the woman is the replica of Mme. Bertin. She throws her scarf and her purse on one of the twin beds.*

THE WOMAN: *(out of breath)* God, these appointments with the hairdresser. I swear, this is the last time. *(She rushes to the wash basin behind the screen and begins washing her hands.)* I love the little lady who takes care of me, she's really a doll. But all those white and balding heads in such a confining space is more than I can handle.

Did anyone come while I was gone? *(No answer.)*

Fernand, are you listening? Did they come for you?

> *Silence except for the water running. The woman closes the faucet, steps out from behind the screen, and at last sees Mme. Bertin slumped in the armchair.*

THE WOMAN: Oh God forgive me. Oh God forgive me if I'm the cause of all this. *(She goes to the door and locks it.)* Did anyone see you?

MME. BERTIN: The usual half-wits.

THE WOMAN: Who?

MME. BERTIN: The little nurse's aide.

THE WOMAN: She doesn't count.

MME. BERTIN: The female doctor.

THE WOMAN: Oh, that one. Did she get close to you?

MME. BERTIN: She took my blood pressure, but she's so scared I'll pop her one when I'm in this state, she pretended not to notice.

THE WOMAN: Anybody else?

MME. BERTIN: The neighbor. You were supposed to go to the hairdresser's together.

THE WOMAN: Rose, Lord yes, I totally forgot. No wonder she gave me such a dirty look.

MME. BERTIN: I told her I didn't feel like going to the hairdresser's.

THE WOMAN: Don't worry about her. She'll never figure it out and nobody would believe her anyway. Any other visits?

MME. BERTIN: The arts and crafts girl.

THE WOMAN: Claire? She's a darling. She understands us. She'll never tell... Fernand, take off the dress.

MME. BERTIN: No.

> *A knock. Then a rattle of the doorknob. An angry voice shouts: "M. Bertin, you are late for the psychologist."*

THE WOMAN: *(crying out)* Coming. *(Urging Mme. Bertin to stand and feverishly beginning to unbutton her)* You're late. Fernand, get dressed. Be reasonable, please. *(Removing Mme. Bertin's dress)* Fernand, darling, please be reasonable.

You promise you won't say anything to the psychologist?

MME. BERTIN: *(removing his wig and jewelry)* Don't worry. I won't say a word.

> *Together they take off his bra, his girdle, his shoes and stockings.*

THE WOMAN: *(frantic, pulling on his trousers while he puts on his shirt)* Not a word? You promise? Just let him talk and don't say anything.

> *The woman grabs tissues and wipes away his makeup while he puts on socks and shoes.*

MME. BERTIN: I promise. And you promise to tell me more?

THE WOMAN: I swear.

MME. BERTIN: How you reached the limits of distress long before I did?

THE WOMAN: Yes, everything.

> *She finishes the transformation by combing his hair. M. Bertin is ready for his appointment.*

MME. BERTIN: Are you scared?

THE WOMAN: I always am when you go to the psychologist's. *(Smiling, she takes his hands in hers.)* You look fine now. Nobody will ever know...

MME. BERTIN: Except our little accomplice, Claire.

THE WOMAN: No one who wishes us harm.

MME. BERTIN: You mean those who want to separate us? No, they'll never know.

> *Footsteps approach the door.*
> *The couple freezes for a moment, facing the audience. Despite the difference in costume, they still look like twins.*
> *There is a resounding knock.*
> *The couple embraces passionately.*

THE WOMAN: You've got to go. Promise me again, Fernand. *(Cupping his face in her hands)* Not a word, you swear.

MME. BERTIN: I swear.

THE WOMAN: They'll lock you up in an asylum and I'll grow old all by myself. Old, you hear.

MME. BERTIN: *(patting her hands)* Never.

THE WOMAN: *(in a sob)* I love you so much it hurts. My heart and my body ache.

MME. BERTIN: *(smiling)* At least you know how to say it.

> *Still sobbing she brings his face to hers and kisses him on the mouth.*

∼

Larry Tremblay

Translated from the French by
Sheila Fischman

UBU REPERTORY THEATER PUBLICATIONS
NEW YORK

Larry Tremblay was born in Chicoutimi, north of Quebec City, in 1954. During his many stays in India over the course of a decade he studied kathakali, and, in 1984, he founded the LAG (Laboratoire gestuel). Among the many plays to which he has contributed as actor or director are *Les Mille grues* and *Le Déclic du Destin,* which he also wrote. Both of these plays represented Canada in 1989 and 1990 at international festivals in Brazil and Argentina. In addition to his work in drama production, he is also a playwright, poet, and essayist. *Leçon d'anatomie (Anatomy Lesson)* was first produced in 1992, at the Théâtre d'Aujourd'hui in Montreal, directed by René Richard Cyr and with Hélène Loiselle in the role of Martha. Larry Tremblay currently heads the Department of Theater at the University of Quebec in Montreal, where he also teaches acting. His newest play, *The Dragonfly of Chicoutimi,* will be co-produced this coming May under his direction by the Festival du Théâtre des Amériques and the Théâtre d'Aujourd'hui.

Sheila Fischman has translated the work of many of Quebec's leading writers, including Anne Hébert, Michel Tremblay, Lise Bissonnette, Roch Carrier, François Gravel and Jacques Poulin. Among other honours, she has twice been presented with the Félix-Antoine Savard Award, given by Columbia University.

The English translation of *Leçon d'anatomie* was made possible thanks to the publications committee of the University of Quebec in Montreal.

For Yoyo

AUTHOR'S NOTE

We are not necessarily born on the day of our birth

You have less than 90 minutes to recount your life. What are you going to extract from your past? What part of your story will you subtract? What other part will you put forward in order that the rest can be deduced? We are not necessarily born on the day of our birth.

Before I knew Martha's story, before I had written the first line of it, I was obsessed by a question: What can one person know about another? How far can you take your knowledge of another before your concern for exactness destroys what you love—at the same time destroying yourself?

Once the first line had been written, my original question was modified but it lost none of its power of amazement: Why is it that we love those who destroy us?

And so Martha was the character who had gone to look for the answer. In order to discover it or to forge it, she did not hesitate to transform her own life into an anatomy lesson—an undertaking that was serious and painful but not without irony and a certain pleasure. You need that when you are opening the stacked-up bodies of your own life and of those who have loved them—or hated them. You need to when you are catching your own conscience as it is about to commit the crime of hatred. And you need it above all when you are about to nullify knowledge in desire.

But how to show this anatomy lesson on stage?

"This man is my husband:" these are Martha's first words. In her declaration, it is the demonstrative pronoun "this" which is intriguing. It shows that Martha is pointing somewhere, physically or mentally, to her husband, that she is showing him to the audience, that she is taking him as a subject to be studied. The entire production follows from that one demonstrative pronoun. Pierre, Martha's husband, is then in a sense present on the stage. He may be an actor or a dummy circumscribed by a more banal, more everyday existence in space and time than is Martha. It is easy to imagine Pierre submerged in his morning ritual: he washes, chooses the clothes he will wear, dons them, observes himself in a mirror, prepares his files for the day. Martha in contrast belongs to night and to the lucidity that sheds light upon it. She takes hold of her husband's activities, extracts them from their context, and presents them to the audience as proof for her demonstration. While *Anatomy Lesson* is first and foremost the expression of a singular individual, it is not necessarily a solo piece.

LARRY TREMBLAY

CHARACTERS

MARTHA, *around 50.*

PIERRE, *Martha's husband, 50, silent role (an actor or a dummy or nothing).*

1. MARTHA + PIERRE = ?

MARTHA
This man is my husband
between us there is a story
but I have my own story too
which is not his

I dislike chronologies
I've never been able
to remember dates from history
rather I've never wanted to memorize them
a waste of time
time is important to me
time but not dates numbers
cardiac arrests that try to stop time
as for me I am on the move
he's not
he is frozen there
you see him standing but deep down
he is seated
he is not so intelligent
as his face might lead you to believe
I have evidence of that
our story has given me plenty
but how can one be fair
how can one avoid being worse than the other
worse than he is
I insist on being sincere
otherwise why open your mouth

I would like to begin
to inaugurate
with some certitudes
my husband's name is Pierre

that perfectly banal name
associated in my mind with the face of a handsome man
has finally assumed its true meaning
Pierre that man that husband
is a stone that weighs on me here
from my sex to my throat
I bear it
and the idea of Pierre is heavier
than Pierre himself
has more consistency
causes more suffocation
than a single minute of his presence
I am not at peace
my blood has formed the memory of Pierre
and circulates his image
through all the circuits of my body

Perhaps you see me before you
clothed in a tissue of lies
cloaked by it
entangled in its folds
like an Arab in her veils
very often my skin is damp
needlessly
thirsty but not knowing for what

My name is Martha
I loathe that name
it does not suit me
nothing about me is compatible
with what I am
my parents made a hideous mistake
by giving me that woman's name
I would have preferred the name of a girl
like Isabelle Luce or Annie

Martha is something limp
that seems to stretch out in space
to stick to the floor
Martha is close to being a fleshy woman
whitish
who cares for who blindly caresses someone who
essentially
is none of her business
all my life I have refused
to fuse with that name
to make my body
the emblem of that name

And so we have
here Pierre
there Martha
between them a verb
to love
Pierre loves Martha
here is an arrow
we make an effort
then reverse
and we obtain
Martha loves Pierre
there is another arrow
a current that is propelled
from one name to the other
it undulates it pitches and tosses
but that verb to love
squeezed in between two images
does it operate the same way
in both directions

My love for Pierre
has been a murder

my own
I look at his eyes
mentally remove his blue irises
detach them to examine his thinking
to see his brain at work
I worm my way into his thoughts
I dream of thinking what he is thinking
at the very moment he is thinking it
and I only arrive at the void

There are very few certitudes
if Pierre is the name of my husband
what is the true name
of my feelings for him
the word "love" has become meaningless
has become a dumping ground
with everything flung in a heap
"to burn with love" "to die of love"
senseless combustion
and yet if I touch Pierre
my body grows warm
as does his
to make love
yes we make something
that we call "love"
but I look around us
and see nothing that has been made
the blank space holds only
an impossible sum
Pierre plus Martha equals
only Pierre and Martha
two names

2. WHAT AM I IN THE PROCESS OF CEASING TO BE?

Look at him
Pierre has a very serious face
a strong jaw
they say it's a sign of determination
at night he grinds his teeth
Pierre is tense
but I am the only one who knows
even he does not know
he has always refused to know himself
to go inside himself
in fact Pierre is always outside
is nothing but surface
you might think he has just two dimensions
that he is the product of a false perspective
so lacking is he in true density
I suspect he has never known anguish
only when he is asleep
does he suffer
and then he clenches his jaws
but that is something he doesn't know

Let us try once again to be lucid
I plant myself opposite him without tensing
I try to slow down my breathing
try not to sweat not to flee
calmly I study Pierre
I see his wrinkles
his graying temples
I take note of time
of fatigue of deposits
why HIM
the question is fatuous but persists
I linger at his teeth they are still white

I gaze at his lips rejecting several adjectives
that hover about him like flies
swollen lips moist lips bitten lips
I want to see simply lips
the flesh of bare lips
without the lie of an adjective
I lift up my gaze to his eyes
Pierre can you see me

I realize there is little we can say
about someone
if we insist on doing so in the present tense
my husband stands my husband weighs
my husband has my husband does
I can't bear this possessive inventory
I could talk about the atoms that compose
the cells of my husband's body
I could reduce them to an anatomical drawing
I could be patient
count his bones count the hairs on his head
count the hairs and the pores of his skin
count the breaths he takes
apply to him a light-sensitive plate
how to talk about that man

Fingers very long white
the hands of a civil servant
very civilized hands
I have always been fascinated by hands
because of the verbs to open and to close
which they use
endlessly switching from one to the other
because of everything that they take that they give
because of the hollow they contain
because of everything one can read there

because of the infinite details one can find there
you see me now manipulating Pierre's hand
as if I were holding a secret
I take it between my own hands
like a small animal
that I hold with the utmost care
so as not to injure it
if I concentrate
I can feel the warmth of the blood
that crepitates under the skin
if I concentrate even harder
I detect the hardness of the bones beneath the skin
if I concentrate harder still
I am able to touch what is secret
his hand has slowly dissolved
sugar in coffee
my own hands contain nothing now
but the taste of Pierre
a naked throbbing
horribly disturbing
a cry that calls out to me

Observe
when my body touches it
it swells
with what

What am I in the process of ceasing to be

I am almost fifty years old
so is Pierre
why must I always add
"so is Pierre"
to whatever I say
it shows a lack of autonomy

yet I am proud
terrifically
those who know me describe me
as self-confident
there are those who think me cold
who politely reproach me
but without pushing it
I have too many good qualities
for them to emphasize one of my flaws
I am so obliging so proper
my husband is a politician
I have got in the habit of being polite
attentive witty cultivated
classic distinguished well-packaged
representative of a sphere that is
"slightly superior"
I know I'm sarcastic
I don't like myself
am too brilliant for that
above all am more intelligent than my husband
which is I am convinced
what keeps me from going into politics
in his place
too often you must be simplistic
must see white here
black there
when you hold power
I prefer to see shades of gray
and to confuse my students with courses
like
*"the distribution of the main centrifugal paths
of the orthosympathetic and the parasympathetic"*
or to publish articles
like

*"reward effects of food via stomach fistula
compared with those of food via mouth"*
Pierre is so transparent
a sheet of plastic
to acknowledge an error
would never occur to him
it is utterly impossible for him
to experience self-doubt

3. MUST A WOMAN ACCEPT FLOWERS FROM HER HUSBAND AFTER HE HAS PRACTICALLY BATTERED HER TO DEATH?

I am obsessed
that man
must get to the end of him
as one gets to the end of the road
not because it is him
but because it is me

Compel myself to obey a cruel discipline
not to speak to Pierre
leave him outside this whole story
what I have to say binds no one but me
I no longer pretend
to be concerned with the truth
I am a taut cord
on the point of firing off its final breath
I see myself as ridiculous vain pointless
because I always love in the same place
always in the same place
until love is worn out
the woman who loves is worn out
the man who is loved is worn out
erosion
that's it
cracks and erosion
nothing more
and then a little noise
some words

Cracks
the first crack
a rainy night
I come back drunk to our "home"

a new experience
and a great moment in my life
a moment that drenches me still
that wets my hair lips dress
I come home
filled with heartbeats
Pierre waiting for me in the kitchen
as if he has guessed
I don't know
let's go on as if
yes he is waiting in the kitchen his mind made up
he has not even taken off his lawyer's tie
a hard knot at the tip of his throat
an unblinking eye
I say nothing
speech dares not enter with me
into this house
I left that behind at the bar or on the street
I have no words feel no urge to speak
nor are there words
in Pierre's expression
a couple marked by silence
by forced silence
by the rule of silence
feet stuck to the clean
but indecent kitchen floor
and the silence triggers everything
it has become so solemn
and Pierre is so still
that I explode
in uncontrollable laughter
which strews broken glass everywhere
shards of my body of my breath
of my hair wet from the rain
I laugh where I stand

nailed
then he comes at me
and beats me with his hands
strikes my face my mouth my laughter
the silence returns
he strikes again
stops
when I start to vomit
then everything stops
I he time
there is a huge crack
in space
irreparable
I look at Pierre
I have never seen him
I have never seen that man
why are we together
in this kitchen

I do something foolish
I straighten his tie

I have lost a tooth
I realize he struck me very hard
I look at myself in the mirror
the pain is delayed
I start to wait for it
to watch it arrive on my skin
I think about the crack I want to scream
but my face does not tear apart

The next day
I love Pierre
with fury with blood with pain
above all with horror

when I see myself love him even more than before
in a way that frightens me
the worst moment in my life
the fact that he struck me
that unimaginable fact
that fact changes nothing
on the contrary
it makes love suspect
I do not want to kill him do not want to leave him
all that remains is for me to loathe myself
to loathe desire
to loathe what is returning to the surface of my body

I think Pierre is ridiculous
when he turns up
holding a little bouquet
how original
what a sense of the proprieties
and what a solemn decision to make
in the life of a woman
must she accept the flowers
that her husband offers her
after he has practically battered her to death
I read somewhere
that man lacks the ability to predict
what he will think in the next second
his brain is a ball machine
you can never predict which ball will turn up
that day I don't know how to react
my face is blue and swollen
my hair wrapped in a towel
and the idiot hiding behind his flowers
has an expression like a child's
must I call my lawyer

I am severed
at the root of my tongue
everything that still seethes
in the cistern of my lungs
no more flowers
no flowers ever again

4. WHY DO PEOPLE WHO KNOW WHAT'S GOING ON STAY IN THEIR ROOMS INSTEAD OF TAKING OVER THE PUBLIC PLACE?

Cracks
in the early days of our marriage
it was Pierre who selected all the furniture
who decided on the colour of the curtains
the bedspread rugs plates telephone
I let him have his way
I realized for the first time in my life
that I am utterly indifferent to objects
I have no opinion I have no views
try as I may
I am absolutely unable
to know if I love or hate
the three little sofas
covered in brown velvet
that Pierre adores more than anything else
I can find in myself no valid reason
for suddenly deciding
that they go perfectly in our living room
I quite simply cannot
take a position
endless discussions
take place on those sofas
I listen to Pierre's arguments
to those of his friends
they are all capable
of flaring up for an idea
of detesting their political opponents
of calling them idiots traitors corrupt
of producing clear definitive positions
on every minor event in the week
of declaring they are deeply scandalized
by the remarks of an editorial writer

do I admire them
they are so amazing
they smoke they drink beer
they have big sweat stains
under their arms
they give one the sense
that something important is going on
in this living room
simply because they have ideas
Martha too drinks smokes sweats but says nothing
she observes analyzes weighs the pros and cons
totally cut off
behind her pseudo-scientific neutrality
everything slips between her fingers
lucidity doesn't pay
why do people who know what's going on
stay in their rooms
instead of taking over the public place

My demented love for Pierre
has anaesthetized me
I am reduced
in spite of all my claims
to being merely a loving wife
pathologically drawn to the same magnetic pole
the same legs the same ass
the same trousers
the same shirts the same stripes
pinstripes
Pierre will only wear
pinstriped shirts
he has a whole collection
a veritable passion
in the morning he opens the closet
and before he makes his choice

takes obvious pleasure
in gazing at
his vast collection of pinstriped shirts
starched on their hangers
his life's obsession
he is convinced
there is nothing more impeccable
than a striped shirt
and since nothing is more important
in politics
than that a thing be impeccable
Pierre likes only impeccable things
like this shirt like this tie
like this belly
firm held in never caught out
like these shoulders
strong straight never slumping
IMPECCABLE
Pierre's favourite word

5. SO YOU'VE STARTED?

I am a strange little girl
at thirteen I devote my life
to raising frogs
there is a river
a very small river
called Rivière aux Rats
I've never seen rats in that river
but in the spring
between the rocks
small pools form
teeming with tadpoles
that I catch in my hands
in my parents' house
in one corner of the cellar
I set up a "research laboratory"
on the walls I hang anatomical drawings
I have a real microscope
a Christmas present when I was twelve
syringes even a scalpel
my cousin brought it
from the hospital where she's a nurse
I am very proud of my instruments
I never tire of cleaning them
arranging them in their cases
hiding them in dresser drawers
like treasures
one day I decide
with my parents' permission
to paint my laboratory
mauve
I put up some shelves
also mauve
where I set the jars conspicuously

so I can observe
my poor tadpoles from the Rivière aux Rats
I only feed them
soda crackers
in fact one of my great discoveries
is that tadpoles eat cracker crumbs
an unexpected scientific discovery
very economical too
with just one cracker
I can feed all my samples
THE STAGES IN THE LIFE OF A FROG
I write that on the notebook
where I meticulously compile my observations
the day the tadpole loses its tail
the day the tadpole has two legs
growing in the back
the day the tadpole has two legs
growing in the front
and the wonderful day
most memorable day of all
when with four brand new legs
it's no longer a tadpole
that with one leap kicks itself out of the water
but a frog
no more cracker crumbs
beginning then
I could never shake off the idea
that life consists of stages
when I look at my own life
it seems to me that everything was already inscribed
in the notebook of my thirteenth year
gains losses pleasures pains
your hands the colour of your eyes
the dress I am wearing tonight
and this hairdo that I hate

this lipstick this nail polish
the ache in my heart
the way I have of looking at you
it is quite horrible
this very clinical very professional
BRAINWASHING
there are those who start to cry
when they think of their childhood
what I do is scream
I hate that thirteen-year-old Martha
who takes herself for Jean Rostand
she is not content to
feed cracker crumbs to tadpoles
Martha has a nobler mission
she must get to the root of things
chase down knowledge wherever it is hidden
BENEATH THE SKIN
I experience a great thrill
when I cut open my first frog
I know that all children are sadists
but it's not all children
who imagine they are advancing science
by systematically dissecting
whatever they can get their hands on
dogs rats cats sparrows
I am so serious so adept
and so determined to see things through to the end
Martha wants to know everything
wants to cut open every skin
every belly every organ
nothing can resist her scientific appetite
I remember very clearly
my terrible doggedness
the day when I dissected my brother's turtle
I had to cut open the carapace with scissors
I am certain that when I open it

I shall find a fabulous treasure
like discovering
the secret entrance to a cave
or digging all the way to China
but I always find the same thing
a ghastly smell
Martha holds her nose
and continues to make progress in the material
THE STAGES
after the animal
we move on to man
after months of efforts
I manage to persuade my parents
to buy me a scale model of a human body
my delight when I gaze at
the hundred pieces I have to assemble
inconceivable indecent
I tremble when I think of it
to make my pleasure last
I put together the skeleton as slowly as possible
memorizing like a prayer
the names of all the bones
radius ulna humerus femur
these names intoxicate me transport me
take me out of my age my sex
I am no longer Martha no longer a girl
I am a memory pursed lips
a pair of eyes a pair of hands
busy attaching organs to a skeleton
the final stage consists of placing it all
inside a transparent plastic mould
on which is finely incised the circulation of the blood
I take the time to paint it
the venous blood in blue the arterial in red
striving to follow every convolution

with the feeling that I am drawing
the map of the secret
the secret that adults hide from children
blue red
the colours of death of life
every time Pierre
that you kissed me
every time I gazed at the blue vein on your forehead
you always closed your eyes while making love
and I always looked at your closed eyes
observing your veins swollen by love
I apologize Pierre
I never had much pleasure with you
I often thought about that scale model
when you came
I never wanted to know why
now I have some idea
no I have no idea
I have always known
Martha always knows everything
THE STAGES
the scale model has a surprise in reserve
has an option
a fetus
the scale model is a woman then
or rather can become one
one need only add on part number 101
I was never able to attach it
a flaw in construction
perfectly in keeping with what I am
if I'd known at the time
that I was present at my own destiny
I would have asked my parents then and there
to return the defective model to the store
and give me another

I am not superstitious I'm not fatalistic
I believe in human freedom
we are not free to live
but at least we are free to die
isn't that so Pierre

I hate this moment of lucidity
I don't like to see myself
in the process of understanding what is happening to me
and I hate to hear myself say so

The defective model
I began to hate myself on the day of my first period
I was late starting
I was over fourteen
and never regular
I would bleed for a whole week
then for months nothing
very soon my sex became a strange object
for expert hands to explore
my mother asks questions
so you've started
studies my sheets my underwear
I burn my notebook filled with observations
and bury alive
a huge frog
along with all my laboratory instruments
for years
Martha does not even pick up a cat
I can't stand to be touched
I compare myself with other
regular girls
I decide to become a saint
I'm obsessed with the life of St. Theresa of Avila
I imagine being uplifted like her

by my love for Jesus Christ
I found countless convents
travel to a thousand countries
meet my nuns my girls my orphans
distribute the accumulated money
received from the wealthy and pious
I build hospitals churches
help priests get established in remote countries
command the admiration of the poor the rich
attract the infirm
hold in my arms dying infants
that my hands bring back to life
all of that takes place in my brain
between seven and eight o'clock
the hour when my mother sends me to bed
I am convinced that she will find me dead there
unless before I go to sleep
I ask God to let me live
I am alienated from a to z
there's not a fragment of my bones
that has not been scoured by fear
I am filled most of all with hatred
intense hatred
that produces odours hot flashes
that makes me vomit at school
that keeps me from crying when my father dies
the first time I saw you Pierre
you struck me as phony
that was when you were reading a book a week
you would jot a few phrases on a card
master the gist of it
then bring it up in every conversation
to me you are horribly pretentious
but you impress everyone else
I am the only one who is aware of your tricks

I don't stand on ceremony I denounce you
I make you a laughing stock
you cannot imagine how much I hate you
how methodical I am
at organizing that hatred
I learn to guess what you are going to say
memorize what you've already said
so I can repeat it when you say the opposite
then I take pity on you
decide you're a weakling with no imagination
but that you have a kind heart
I disparage you and you become small
too small Pierre too accessible to everyone
so then I no longer have a choice
I defend you support your points of view
criticize your opponents
I have an urge to caress your hands
I was wrong that's obvious
the young lawyer so brilliant so destined for success
I wait for you to take me you do so
I am fascinated by your ability to fall asleep
with no transition
while I spend hours
spying on you as you sleep
I tell myself you are a force a true force
you sleep you eat you think you come
without the slightest effort
unquestionably I am lying
beside a perfect man
beside you Martha is so flawed
plunged in the darkness of your breathing

6. WHY AM I STILL LIVING BESIDE HIM WITH THIS MOUTH THAT TALKS?

Drawers
I have drawers everywhere
pile in everything
wounds blood
last year's broken arm
there are times when it becomes unreal
to think that none of it has ever existed
feel as if I am inventing it to distract myself
work
of course there is work
Martha the specialist in behaviorism
the head the obligatory reference
to understand criticize surpass
the theory of animal and human behaviour
KNOWLEDGE
another drawer a trap
like politics
everything has been said
revised and corrected
clichés clichés
yet it is so effective
the man is a mouse
the man has pleasure or the man is afraid
sugar cube or electric shock
the only choice of the man
condemned to answer with a yes or a no
to laugh or cry
to salivate over emptiness
to love someone
because he associated him with a small childish pleasure
we are all doomed
to die amid sugar and fear

doomed to react dumbly like a muscle
that twitches because it has been pricked
and Martha twitches like a heart before Pierre
Pierre doomed to wear pinstriped shirts

I have often imagined this scene
Pierre is assisting me in a class
he's a puppet
a mannequin transported on castors
the parts of his body are movable retractable
no that's wrong
he is first and foremost alive
I teach
an introductory class something simple
I am very well dressed
as usual in fact
Pierre enters the classroom
I break off what I was saying
I look at him
the students think he's come to the wrong place
or that he's come to announce something important
or that he is the new director
something it doesn't matter what
you go immediately to the small rostrum
and it is THERE that you become a puppet
Pierre stops breathing stiffens
the castors appear
his body is divided up broken into sections
that are coloured according to the organs
his clothes have ALMOST disappeared
the students readily accept
Pierre as he is
I take the ruler
I point aha aha
expound analyze indicate

show reveal what I like what I do not
mark Pierre demarcate the sections
the HEART of Pierre
does his blood conceal images of me
if I opened you up spread open your flesh
would I see something more
than your surface displays
I turn towards the students
they pay close attention
the puppet fascinates them
what they must know about him
simple things
distance
if I position myself a few feet from him
like this
I am no longer sure about anything
but if on the other hand I walk away
like this
there's a chance I would start to love him again
but if I am very close to him like this
his gaze hurts me
I feel that I am going back to him
just as at the end of every line
the typewriter returns to the margin
Pierre's CLOTHES
you dress him in a T-shirt shorts sneakers
he starts to tan before your eyes
naked Pierre disappears completely
Pierre's SEX
must I weave a few phrases
around this organ
translate the experience of sex into opinions
into declarations evaluations
show myself to be intransigent precise
to present as they say a dissertation

a dissertation on the sex life of Pierre and Martha
on the two of them when they copulate
the word copulate is filled with horror
I copulate does that make sense
I know copulate does not exist
nor does to make love
Pierre and I have intercourse
Pierre's HANDS
that's what men in politics
offer most easily
whenever I see you on television
giving your opinion on the latest scandal
I always observe what they are doing
I know when they lie
or rather when they denounce you
they fascinate me I've said so I've said so
now let us move on to the essential
Pierre's STOMACH
I turn towards a student
I order her
no I ask her to stand to come closer
to lift your abdomen to extract the stomach from it
to display it to the class to explain why
to hide nothing of the truth
to say everything omit nothing
to take as much time as necessary to explain
in all its details in all its subtleties
emphasizing the most important words
why yes why
this man this rock that oppresses me
beats what is still called his wife
to explain with the necessary words
why this woman Martha
is still living beside him
with this mouth that talks talks

7. WHY GOOD LUCK?

Martha accumulates facts
not dates I've said so I've said so
I don't like dates
facts Pierre for example
has never forgiven me for the fact
that I am sterile
that I have had a breast amputated
that I have published four scientific books
that I have received an award
and so on and so on and so on
one date however only one
the night of November 15
unforgettable for both of us
Pierre has lost his voice
from shouting too hard his joy
his slogans his love of man
as for me I am rather cold to it all
for good reason I am in the hospital
the next day they will cut off my breast
you phone me
good luck
why good luck
you could have told me I love you I'm with you
you hang up
they give me a sleeping pill
I fall asleep my head filled with
your idiotic good luck
which after many repetitions
I hear as good for the trash heap
good for the trash heap
Pierre on the day
I am officially declared
incapable of having children

demands at once that I dress
in keeping with his own frustration
more and more jewels more perfume more packaging
more "Martha you're amazing you look younger every day"
more "behind every great man there's a woman"
Pierre your wife never voted for you
I never dared admit it to you never
I do not share your political goals
your vision
I do not support your way of thinking
which I find infinitely childish
I have not told you
how bigoted I think you are
I listen to you talk about immigration
in the new society that will exist in the year 2000
about the next century that will belong to us
about your design your design for society
you talk about it with such conviction
but you always refused to adopt a child
always refused even to talk about it
state secret the matter is closed

CRACKS
cracks and erosion

My lost breast
I picture it rotting
in the hospital garbage
I place a mouth where it no longer is
and cry out
I open the wound
and I cry out for it to come back
I remember everything clearly
the first time you take off the bandage
that you dare

that you place a finger on the pain
then the day when you look at yourself in the mirror
at what is left of you
the care you take to avoid opening the wound
the time you spend observing it
noting its progress
your anxiety as you try to find the *mot juste*
disgust pity hatred tenderness
astonishment at losing
a piece of yourself
without losing your mind
and then that look in your eyes your silence
the time it takes you to undress
to fold your clothes to put them away
to remove your watch
to wash to prepare yourself
to tremble to hide your trembling
your gaze that lights everywhere
on the furniture the walls
the glint of the mirror in the shadows
the bed the open sheets me
the desire that awaits
comes goes
the panic the acts
the acts

The silence the silence
MASTECTOMY
after that banal and horrible operation
after the even more horrible treatments
I must submit to
after the loss of my hair
of my appetite my energy
after your attitude even more horrible
than the treatments and losses

I lose control of my life altogether
stop working
have no interest in anything
opening my eyes in the morning
noting that it is Martha who is opening them
is the most painful part of the day
I have stopped calling anyone
colleagues relatives friends
I no longer wish to see them
the very thought of their existence
is intolerable
in fact I can no longer tolerate anything
especially the furniture curtains paintings
everything that the couple has
slowly painfully lovingly
accumulated over the years
all the thousands of stupid useless objects
that have multiplied savagely
behind their backs underfoot
Martha can no longer tolerate them
I take an apartment
alone
a totally empty apartment
white walls white ceilings
bare windows
the echo of silence
the sound of my footsteps on the floor
no telephone
CRACKS
I write that in big letters
on the wall that faces
the single bed I've just bought
one week later
there are hundreds of CRACKS on the wall
tangled illegible

they look at me terrify me
there are also drawings of plans
curves numbers arrows
and two names
Pierre and Martha
I am less and less able to tolerate the silence
which I manufacture from my odours
my sleep my movements
with the three or four dresses
I can still wear
more and more obsessed
with the word CRACK
that repeats itself within me
and I cannot silence it
I buy a dictionary
and write on the wall
all the examples that pertain to the word
If from this broken breast pain and ecstasy
should pour out like water from the cracks in a vase
Victor Hugo *Songs at Dusk*
She has sounded
my sensitivity so deeply
that I have applied putty to the cracks
and because of that she vibrates less
Flaubert
We maintain that lovers' quarrels
renew love
in reality they create cracks
that nothing resolves
Montherlant
Her birth had been only a crack
that grew bigger over time
Martha

8. WHAT DID YOU SAY?

Then everything is turned upside down
moves too fast
for me to stop anything whatsoever
this speed of things of deeds of thoughts
I have never felt within myself
such speed
but also such a void
now everything I do is done
with an incredible emptiness
I bring home a mannequin
head torso limbs
a store-window dummy
nude pink male without a sex
that I assemble dress
red pinstriped shirt blue three-piece suit
brown polished shoes ochre yellow socks
neckties
I buy two ties
a red one a blue
choose the blue one
then change my mind put on the red
I position the clothed mannequin
in the middle of the living room
it stands there in the centre of the emptiness
surrounded by the white walls
I walk around him several times
adjust the crease in the trousers
re-do the knot in the necktie
re-button the jacket
loosen the belt by a notch
position myself opposite him
stare him in the eyes
wait wait for a very long time

Speed
it returns
once again deeds are turned upside down
with more force with more emptiness
everything must be started fresh
I bring home other mannequins
dress them move them observe them
there is one in the kitchen
feet glued to the floor
another is seated
head bowed hands on the table
another in the bathroom
another seen from behind
stands in one corner of the bedroom
another hidden in the closet
the apartment is full of them
all of them impeccable
save for the one in the kitchen
he is missing one hand

Then everything is jolted again
I undress a mannequin
lay him in the bed
pull the sheet up to his head
wait watch
pull the sheet down to his feet
sit him up lay him down
cover him completely with the sheet

Time passes
a long time

It is dark in the apartment
slowly I undress
lift the sheet get into bed

I have a nightmare
we are together
in the same bed
between us there is a corpse
I am astonished that it's there
you're not
I try to see the face
I approach it closer closer
and just as I am about to catch sight of it
I waken
the sheets are wet I get up
switch on all the lights in the apartment
I cannot stay in the bed
I am afraid of the bed of the mannequin
Pierre that night I could have killed myself
the conditions were quite favourable
a neurotic woman sick filled with anguish
alone with a cabinet full of drugs
all I needed to do was to leave
conspicuously on the kitchen table
a farewell letter
already written dozens of times
aha aha Martha is dead
better that way
it solves all the problems
or again
what good timing
it couldn't have worked out better
the world is not so badly made after all
there is always a solution
just had to think of it
all things must end
aha aha all's well that ends well

I put on jeans a heavy sweater

the wig I bought during the treatments
that I never had the courage to wear
I blast it all with perfume
totally disguised
I go out
for the first time in months
as if I'd been ashamed to show myself
as if someone might recognize me
I am playing a trick but on whom
I do not exist I incite nothing
I go into a cinema
buy popcorn coke
two things I can't stand
I cannot bear either the smell
or the sound they make
I don't know what I'm going to see
the film starts I'm disappointed
an infantile American movie
car-chase shoot-out
it's supposed to be hilarious and it is
the audience laughs at every gag I don't
two blocks away
I go into another cinema
the film has already begun
I don't know if it's the beginning middle or end
very quickly I realize it doesn't matter
ten minutes later
Martha has already assumed her serious look
the scientist she has become again
appreciates the clarity of the words
the simplicity of the demonstration
and the effectiveness of its repetition
there is only one thing to show
there is only one thing to do
beside me a man is caressing himself

I feel a pain in my breast
the one I no longer have
Pierre I don't love you any more
I am no longer watching the film
I stare at the red letters
above the emergency door
EXIT the word beckons me
he has spotted me
the man is stroking my thighs
I want to laugh
drawers Martha has drawers everywhere
but they're empty
the man works his hand under my sweater
I do not look at him
keep staring at the red letters
he caresses my belly
I think about absurd things
to go back to teaching
agree to conduct that seminar in Washington
buy a country house
his hand is blazing hot
he tries to slip it between my thighs
is unsuccessful moves it up
tries to work it under my bra
I hear myself tell him
I am not impeccable
what did you say I AM NOT IMPECCABLE
before I realize that I have just screamed
I am standing up holding my wig
opening the door to the emergency exit
the anatomy lesson is over
I am in a dark alley
rain is falling there are puddles everywhere
I run not knowing where I am going
emerge in a closed courtyard

hear myself screaming again
I AM NOT IMPECCABLE
turn around
step into the same puddles
finally find the sidewalk
the first thing I do
is to check that I still do not love you
the brief moment of panic
I have just lived through
has made me lose my train of thought
I am reassured it holds fast
I am still carrying my wig
I throw it away cross the street go into a café
the first thing I see is you
smiling idiotically at me
from the cover of a newsmagazine
THE NEW QUEBECOIS HAS ARRIVED
four pages about you two colour photos
all at once I laugh like a lunatic
but as I read the article I want to weep
you are being sanctified during your lifetime
with ready-made phrases
this fifty-year-old
younger than ever
personifies the future
he likes to say
the past that's not for me
or again
his ideas but above all his charm
readily win him the women's vote
I am mentioned
just once in the article
an insipid remark
absolutely devoid of love or meaning
Pierre tells the journalist

my wife's cancer has made me reflect about
the precarious nature of every situation
that is all
Pierre says nothing else about "his wife"
The Honourable Minister does not deem it necessary
to add another word
to his dazzling observation
I admire the spirit of synthesis
the conciseness
fourteen words I counted them three times
with which you make use of MY cancer
to reflect about the world
what stops you from reflecting about me
if you could strike me from your life
by signing some form
you would do it
I have become a burden
too slow for history
too heavy for the future
that you embody so well according to the polls
now I understand your relief
when I told you I wanted to live alone
you did not seem surprised shocked scandalized
no
only relieved
you thought it perfectly normal
that a woman in my condition
should decide to leave "the comforts of home"
to live out her cancer on her own
what a splendid idea after all
you could have protested held me back
taken me in your arms struck me
as you are in the habit of doing
nothing
only relief

I close the magazine
you continue to smile at me
from the cover
something is not quite right
your face is different
I study the forehead the eyes the lips the teeth
I know what's wrong
I no longer recognize Martha in your expression
she has flown away
the photo shows you at your desk
dressed to the nines
hands clasped
resting on a stack of files
your hands are bare
no wedding ring
I notice a tear dropping onto them
then another
I am devastated
Martha is crying Martha is producing tears
that will wash up
on the glossy paper of your photo
this is the height of the ridiculous
the summit of foolishness has been surpassed
the tears I refused to shed
even your blows had not caused them to well up
even the announcement of my death
had not shaken them loose
are flowing now in this seedy café
with no concern for me
they pass through me
without asking my permission
carrying with them the words
that my body will never utter again

When I return to the apartment
after this first outing
after this memorable abortive evening at the movies
another woman walks in my shoes
takes a taxi mounts the stairs
undresses climbs into bed
another woman is there at dawn
before a wall full of graffiti and children's drawings
where she reads a phrase
that she now understands for the first time
THE STAGES IN THE LIFE OF A FROG

9. MARTHA - PIERRE = ?

There you have it
I am here
before you
alive

We have
here Pierre
and there Martha
between the two
erosion
erosion so intense
that even space is eroded

I stand upright before him
my gaze travels
to these lips these shoulders
to that upraised hand
I can say ridiculous things
such as
if he really loves me
that love should shine from his eyes
fill the space
cause the appearance of
furniture plants curtains
but I do not say so

Every time Pierre
that you kissed me
every time I gazed at the blue vein on your forehead.

~